Adventures in
KNITTING

Adventures in
KNITTING

More than 100 Patterns, from Easy to Intricate

———————◆———————

BARBARA AYTES

1968

Doubleday & Company, Inc.

Garden City, New York

PHOTOGRAPHY

Pattern stitches and knitted items throughout (except as noted below) by Jerome Shapiro, Van Nuys, California
Photos on pages 4, 6, 9, 25, 71, 88, by D. Waggoner, Granada Hills, California

FASHION MODEL

Dede Boggs, Malibu Canyon, California

MODEL FOR DOG WALKING COAT on page 25

Timmy Worfolk, Reseda, California

Giant machines, powered by electricity and controlled by push buttons, turn out knitted items by the untold millions each year, quickly made and cheaply priced; but the machine has not been invented that can give these fabrics a handmade look. In every corner of the earth there are those who still prefer a handmade fabric, knitted in the same manner as it was before Queen Anne was born, for it requires more than a mere machine to put the look of fine workmanship into a knitted pattern; this can be done only by human hands and creative hearts.

How to Use This Book

While some of the patterns in these pages are older than the printed page and others were formulated and became favorites during the Victorian era, a large number were designed by the author especially for this book and are so new that you may be the first to put them to practical or decorative use.

The patterns in Section I are, as the title indicates, smart and simple. Smart enough for the most advanced knitter, either as they are or combined with other more elaborate designs—and simple enough for the beginner.

In all probability, a beginner using this book will already have been taught the basics such as knit, purl, over, cast on, and bind off. It is assumed, however, that occasionally even an advanced knitter will encounter an action of the knitting needles that she has never seen before or has used so little as to require a memory refresher. So for the beginner and the advanced knitter alike, General Instructions are given on pages 169–179, giving clear, step-by-step directions for working any stitch or execution of the knitting needles encountered in the following pages, including all the basics.

It is suggested that knitters who are unfamiliar with pattern stitches begin by first perusing the General Instructions and then start their pattern knitting with some of the two- or four-row directions, such as Baby Diamond, Signe, Moss Stitch, or other simple designs with familiar background stitches. Beginning pattern knitting in this way will delight and encourage the novice, and before long she will find herself happily and easily using the most intricate of the fabric designs.

Section II is entitled "Unique and Unusual." Beginners and advanced knitters alike will revel in patterns having such unlikely names as Checkerboard Bows, Frills and Pearls, Dragonfly Border, and Peruvian, while the far-out knitters, in all probability, will run rampant (with a pair of knitting needles) through Treva, Embossed Shell, Bellflower and Cable, and others of the brand-new designs in this second collection.

Although Section III is called "Intricate and Elegant," the word "intricate" refers primarily to the effect of the designs upon the eye of the beholder and not necessarily to the directions of the patterns. While a few are somewhat intricate in execution, most of them are such that a semiadvanced knitter will have no trouble using them, and some, in spite of the section title, are simple enough for the slightly advanced beginner.

The knitter will find in this group a collection of those patterns which yield a maximum of design for a minimum of effort. There are many hundreds of patterns extant that are quite the opposite, yielding a minimum of pattern for a maximum of effort. Most of these involve working complicated stitches on the reverse side as well as the front of the fabric, and often involve thirty or forty rows. In the opinion of the author, most of these patterns, while attractive, simply do not yield enough design to warrant the many rows and the enormous amount of concentration required. The very few of these that have been included have been simplified and modified as much as possible and are, in their present form, well worth the effort.

Whether the knitter wishes to try the designs that involve many pattern rows and lesser known stitches or prefers to stay with the more familiar and shorter directions, she will find that they all contain elements of fascinating design and are elegant however they are used—and elegance, like virtue, is its own reward.

Contents

ILLUSTRATIONS

PHOTOGRAPHS

DIAGRAMS

I
SMART AND SIMPLE

BABY DIAMOND

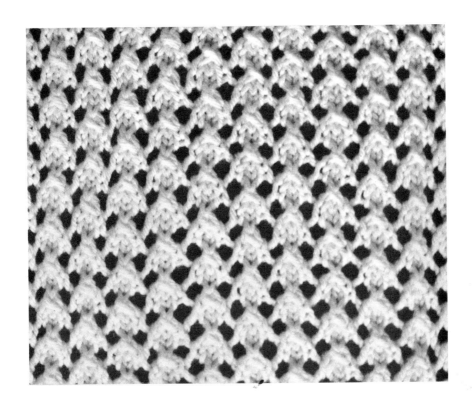

Cast on a multiple of 6 stitches plus 2.

Row 1: K 1, *k 3, o, sl 1, k 2 tog, psso, o*. Repeat between *'s across row and end last st: K 1.

Row 2: Purl across row, purling each over (o) as a separate st.

Row 3: K 1, *o, sl 1, k 2 tog, psso, o, k 3*. Repeat between *'s across row and end last st: K 1.

Row 4: Same as Row 2.

ISABEL

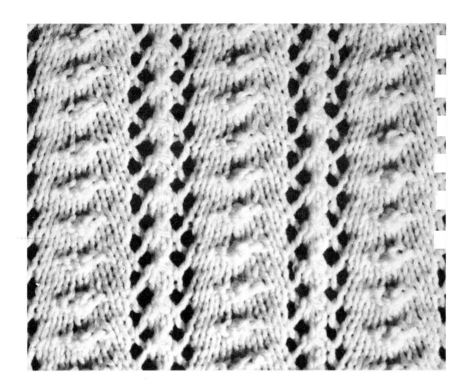

Cast on a multiple of 12 stitches plus 1.

Row 1: K 5, *o, sl 1, k 2 tog, psso, o, k 9*. Repeat between *'s across row → and end last repeat: K 5 (instead of k 9).
Row 2: Purl.
Row 3: P 3, *k 2, o, k 3, o, k 2, p 5*. Repeat between *'s across row → and end last repeat: P 3 (instead of p 5).
Row 4: K 2 tog, *p 11, k 3 tog*. Repeat between *'s across row → and end last repeat: K 2 tog (instead of k 3 tog).

OLD SHALE

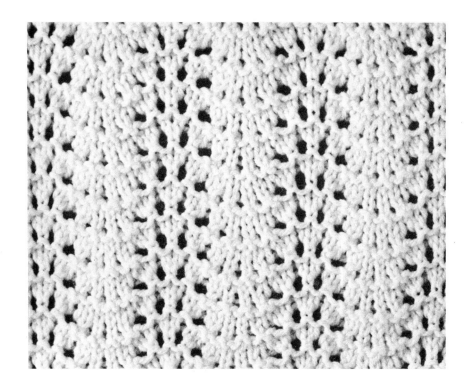

Cast on a multiple of 11 stitches.

Row 1: *K 2 tog, k 2 tog, o, (k 1, o) 3 times, k 2 tog, k 2 tog*. Repeat between *'s across row.

Row 2: Purl across row, purling each over (o) as a separate stitch.

Row 3: Knit across row.

Row 4: Knit across row.

LILITH

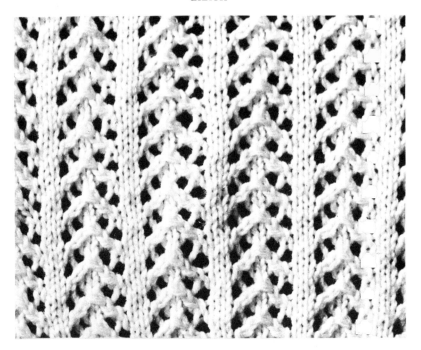

SIGNE

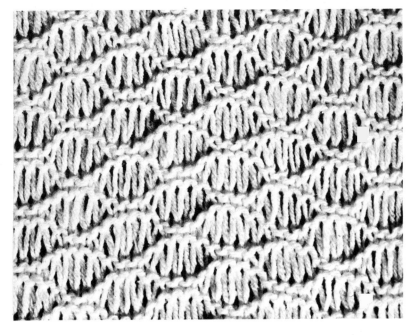

LILITH

Cast on a multiple of 7 stitches.

Row 1: *K 1, o, sl 1, k 1, psso, k 1, k 2 tog, o, k 1*. Repeat between *'s across row (bearing in mind that each repeat begins and ends with a k 1).
Row 2: Purl.
Row 3: *K 2, o, sl 1, k 2 tog, psso, o, k 2*. Repeat between *'s across row (bearing in mind that each repeat begins and ends with a k 2).
Row 4: Purl.

SIGNE

Cast on a multiple of 8 stitches.

Row 1: *K 4, knit a triple throw into each of next 4 sts*. Repeat between *'s across row.
Row 2: Knit, knitting the first strand of each triple throw and dropping the second and third strands.
Row 3: *Knit a triple throw into each of next 4 sts, k 4*. Repeat between *'s across row.
Row 4: Repeat Row 2.

SUMMER STOLE in Signe Pattern

Materials required: 4 4-oz skeins 4-ply knitting worsted, 1 pair ⚹9 knitting needles

Stitch gauge: 8 sts equal 2″.

Cast on 80 sts and work in Signe Pattern until stole measures approximately 70″ from beginning (or desired length). Complete pattern through Row 3, then bind off all sts (knitwise) on reverse side of fabric loosely.

BERRY PATCH

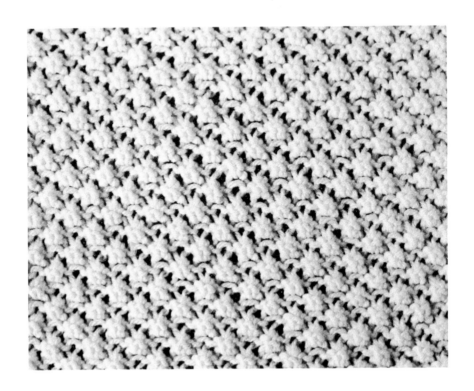

Cast on a multiple of 4 stitches.

Row 1: K 2, *(k 1, p 1, k 1) into next st (making 3 sts from the 1), p 3 tog*. Repeat between *'s across row and end: K 2.
Row 2: Purl.
Row 3: K 2, *p 3 tog, (k 1, p 1, k 1) into next st*. Repeat between *'s across row and end: K 2.
Row 4: Purl.

LATTICE

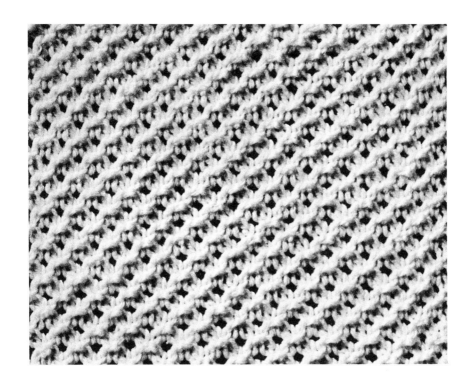

Cast on a multiple of 6 stitches plus 3.

Row 1: K 2, *o, k 3, insert needle into third st on RIGHT needle, lift over first 2 sts and off needle*. Repeat between *'s and end: K 1.
Row 2: Knit.
Row 3: K 1, *k 3, lift third st off right needle (as in Row 1), o*. Repeat between *'s across row and end: K 2.
Row 4: Knit.

AUSTRIAN PUFF

There are several versions of this, dating back to the late Victorian era, all of substantially the same appearance in spite of different multiples and varying directions.

Cast on a multiple of 11 stitches plus 1.

Row 1: K 1, *o, k 3, k 2 tog, k 2 tog, k 3, o, k 1*. Repeat between *'s across row.
Row 2: Purl.
Row 3: Knit.

MISSY

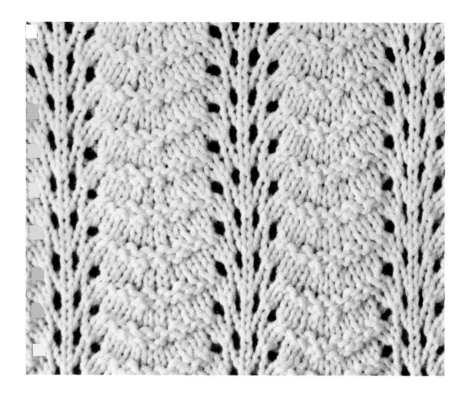

Cast on a multiple of 15 stitches.

Row 1: Purl.

Row 2 (right side): P 5, *k 1, (o, k 1) 4 times, p 10*. Repeat between *'s across row → and end last repeat: P 5 (instead of p 10).

Row 3: K 2 tog, k 2 tog, *p 11, (k 2 tog) 4 times*. Repeat between *'s across row and → end last repeat: K 2 tog, k 2 tog.

Row 4: Knit.

HORIZONTAL STRIPE

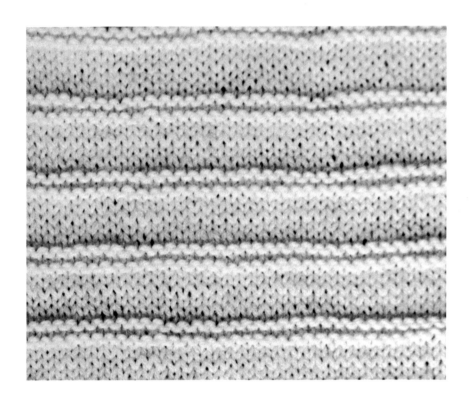

Cast on any number of stitches.

Rows 1, 2, and 3: Knit.
Row 4: Purl.
Row 5: Knit.
Row 6: Purl.
Row 7: Knit.
Row 8: Knit.

MADELON

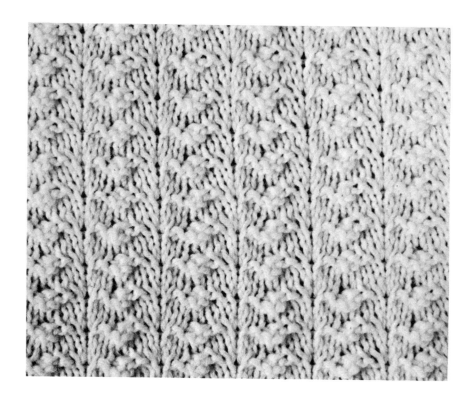

Cast on a multiple of 6 stitches plus 1.

Row 1: Knit.

Row 2: Purl.

Row 3: P 3, *knit a double closed increase into next st, p 5*. Repeat between *'s across row and → end last repeat: P 3 (instead of p 5).

Row 4: K 2 tog, *p 5, k 3 tog*. Repeat between *'s across row → and end last repeat: K 2 tog (instead of k 3 tog).

BASKET WEAVE

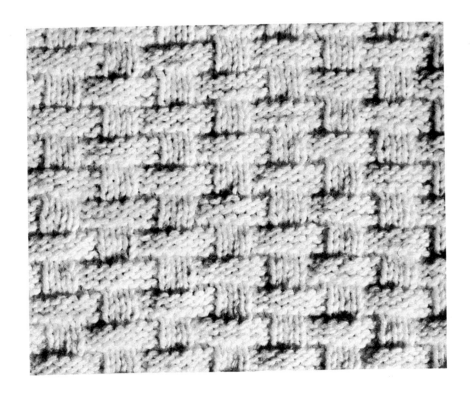

Cast on a multiple of 10 stitches plus 3.

Row 1: *K 3, p 7*. Repeat between *'s across row and end: K 3.

Row 2: *P 3, k 7*. Repeat between *'s across row and end: P 3.

Row 3: Same as Row 1.

Row 4: Purl.

Row 5: P 5, *k 3, p 7*. Repeat between *'s across row → and end: P 5 (instead of p 7).

Row 6: K 5, *p 3, k 7*. Repeat between *'s across row → and end: K 5 (instead of k 7).

Row 7: Same as Row 5.

Row 8: Purl.

CHESSBOARD

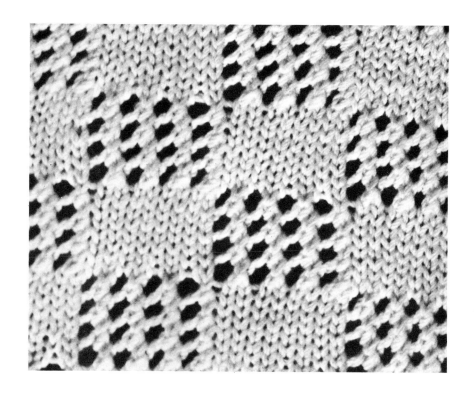

Cast on a multiple of 16 stitches plus 3.

Row 1: K 2, *(o, sl 1, k 1, psso) 4 times, k 8*. Repeat between *'s across row and end: K 1.

Row 2 (and all even-numbered rows): Purl.

Rows 3, 5, and 7: Same as Row 1.

Row 9: K 2, *k 8, (o, sl 1, k 1, psso) 4 times*. Repeat between *'s across row and end: K 1.

Rows 11, 13, and 15: Same as Row 9.

Row 16: Purl.

INGRID

Cast on a multiple of 12 stitches plus 1.

Row 1: P 2, *k 2 tog, k 2, o, k 1, o, k 2, sl 1, k 1, psso, p 3*. Repeat between *'s across row → and end last repeat: P 2 (instead of p 3).
Row 2: Purl.
Row 3: P 2, *k 2 tog, k 1, o, k 3, o, k 1, sl 1, k 1, psso, p 3*. Repeat between *'s across row → and end last repeat: P 2 (instead of p 3).
Row 4: Purl.

GIRL'S CARDIGAN AND CAP SET
in Ingrid Pattern

Materials required: 2 4-oz skeins 4-ply knitting worsted, 1 ✳00 crochet hook, 4 ½″ pearl buttons, and

1 pair ✳8 knitting needles	for age size 2–3
1 pair ✳9 knitting needles	for age size 4–5

Stitch gauge: ✳8 needles, 4½ stitches equal 1″ of pattern stitch.
✳9 needles, 8½ stitches equal 2″ of pattern stitch.

BACK: Cast on 49 sts and work in Ingrid Pattern until fabric measures 7″. Shape sleeves: Cast on 12 sts at beginning of every row (both front and reverse sides of fabric) for next 4 rows, keeping in pattern throughout. (This will make a total of 24 sts added to each side.) Continue in pattern over these 97 sts until piece measures 12″ from beginning of work. Bind off all sts loosely.

LEFT FRONT: Cast on 25 sts and work in pattern stitch for 7″. Shape left sleeve: with right side of fabric facing, cast on 12 sts every other row (1 side only) 2 times. (There will now be 24 added sts on 1 side for left sleeve). Work in pattern over these 49 sts until piece measures 10″ from beginning of work. Shape neck: With reverse side of fabric facing (opposite side from sleeve) bind off 6 sts. Continuing in pattern, and at beginning of every other row, K2 tog (at neck edge only) until 37 sts remain. Continue in pattern until piece measures 12″ from beginning of work and bind off all sts loosely.

RIGHT FRONT: Make as for left front, except: Cast on sts for sleeve with reverse side of fabric facing (opposite side from left front) and bind off sts for neck with right side of fabric facing (opposite side from left front).

COLLAR: Cast on 70 sts and work in k 1, p 1 ribbing for 3½". Bind off all sts.

CUFF (make 2): Cast on 38 sts and work in k 1, p 1 ribbing for 2". Bind off all sts.

Sew shoulder and upper sleeve seams; sew bound-off edges of cuffs to sleeve edges. Sew underarm and side seams. Beginning at center back of neck, work 2 rows of single crochet around entire edge of jacket. On third row, work 4 buttonholes on right center front edge (as in illustration) evenly spaced from neck to within 2" of lower edge. Work 2 more rows of single crochet around entire edge of jacket. Sew buttons on left center front edge to correspond to buttonholes. Block to exact measurements.

MATCHING CAP: Cast on 86 sts and work in k 1, p 1 ribbing for 2", and on last ribbing row knit the last 2 sts tog. Work in Ingrid Pattern for 7"; work should measure 9" in all, including ribbing. Break yarn 18" from work, thread end through yarn needle and run yarn needle through all sts on knitting needle, remove knitting needle, and pull these sts tog snugly. Fasten securely on reverse side, then sew up side edges of cap.

DEDE

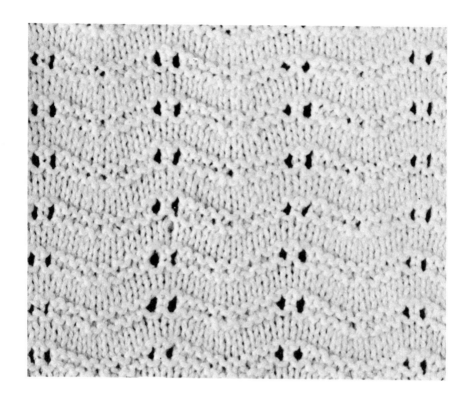

Cast on a multiple of 11 stitches.

Row 1: *K 2 tog, k 3, o, k 1, o, k 3, k 2 tog*. Repeat between *'s across row.
Row 2: Knit.
Row 3: Knit.
Row 4: Purl.
Row 5: Knit.
Row 6: Knit.

NIPPER

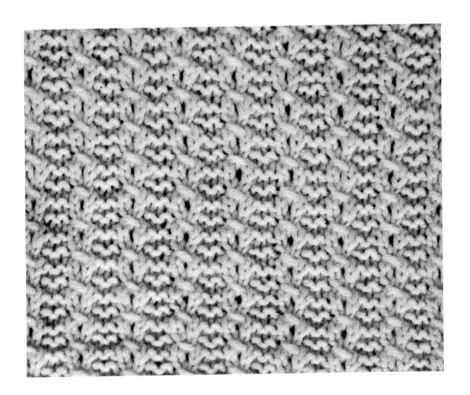

Cast on a multiple of 4 stitches plus 2.

Row 1: P 2, *k 1, o, k 1, p 2*. Repeat across row.
Row 2: Purl.
Row 3: P 2, *sl 1, k 2, psso these 2 sts, p 2*. Repeat across row.
Row 4: Purl.

DONNA

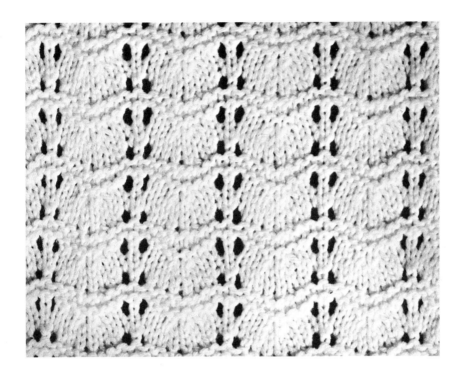

Cast on a multiple of 9 stitches.

Rows 1 and 2: Knit.
Row 3: *K 2 tog, k 2, o, k 1, o, k 2, k 2 tog*. Repeat between *'s across row (bearing in mind that each repeat begins and ends with a k 2 tog).
Row 4: Purl.
Row 5: Knit.
Row 6: Purl.
Row 7: Same as Row 3.
Row 8: Knit.

EYELET CHEVRON

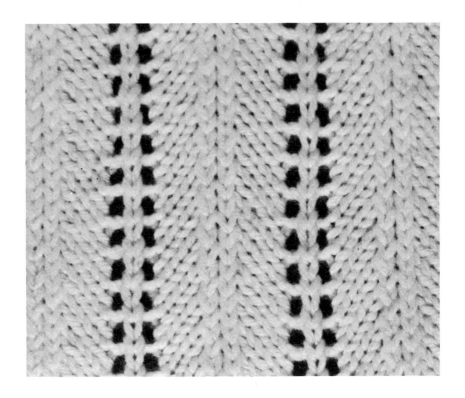

A very simple yet extremely attractive pattern that is undoubtedly one of the oldest, dating well back before the middle ages.

Suggested uses: Women's wear, afghans, mufflers, scarves, stoles, coverlets, baby items

Cast on a multiple of 11 stitches plus 1.

Row 1: K 1, *o, k 3, k 2 tog, sl 1, k 1, psso, k 3, o, k 1*. Repeat between *'s across row.
Row 2: Purl across row.

BATTERSEA

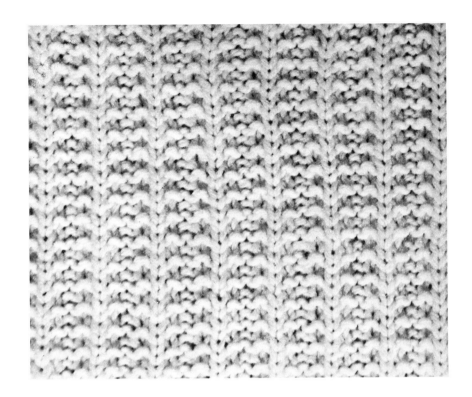

This pattern is sometimes called Broken Rib. A very old pattern and simple enough for any beginner.

Suggested uses: Men's wear, caps, socks, slippers, mufflers, alternating afghan strips

Cast on a multiple of 4 stitches plus 1.

Row 1: *K 3, p 1*. Repeat between *'s across row and end: K 1.
Row 2 (reverse side): Same as Row 1.

DOUBLE PURL

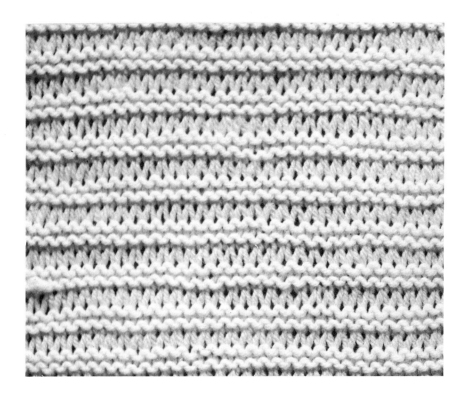

Cast on any number of stitches.

Row 1: Knit.
Row 2: Knit.
Row 3: Knit a double throw into each st across row.
Row 4: Knit across row, inserting right needle into first strand of each st and knitting as usual, slipping second strand from left needle without working.

WALKING COAT for Dog or Cat in Double Purl Pattern

Materials required: 1 4-oz skein 4-ply knitting worsted, 5 flat ½″ buttons, 1 ✗00 crochet hook, 1 pair ✗8 knitting needles

Stitch gauge: 8 sts equal 2″.

Directions are given for a cat or small dog size; directions are in parentheses for medium and large dog.

Cast on 28 sts (32 sts, 36 sts) and work in Double Purl Pattern. Increase 1 st each side on Rows 1 and 2 of pattern stitch until there are 36 sts (44 sts, 50 sts) on needles. Continue in pattern without further increases until work measures 1″ LESS than the exact length of back of animal, measured from base of tail to shoulder. Measure work lying flat on a firm surface, and smoothed out lengthwise as much as possible. On next Row 1 of pattern, knit across 14 sts (16 sts, 17 sts), bind off next 8 sts (12 sts, 16 sts) for neckline and knit across remaining sts. Work each shoulder separately, as follows: Work in pattern over shoulder, decreasing 1 st at neck edge (only) every other row until 11 sts (13 sts, 15 sts) remain. Continue in pattern without further decreases until shoulder section measures 2½″ (3″, 4″) and bind off all sts loosely. Attach yarn at neck edge on opposite shoulder and work the same. Single crochet around entire coat, working 3 single crochet sts in each corner of shoulder pieces each round. On second round, work 3 buttonholes on bound-off edge of right shoulder, evenly spaced, then complete third round of crochet. Underside button tab: Chain 8 (10, 12), turn, single crochet in each chain, *turn, ch 1; sgl cr in each st across row*, repeat between *'s until tab measures 2″ (2¾″, 3½″). Work 2 buttonholes on next row; work 1 more row. Sew tab to underside center on right side. Sew buttons at neck and underside to correspond to buttonholes.

CHECKER

Cast on a multiple of 6 stitches plus 3.

Row 1: *K 3, p 3*. Repeat between *'s across row, and end: K 3.
Row 2: *P 3, k 3*. Repeat between *'s across row, and end: P 3.
Row 3: Same as Row 1.
Row 4: Same as Row 1.
Row 5: Same as Row 2.
Row 6: Same as Row 1.

MOSS STITCH

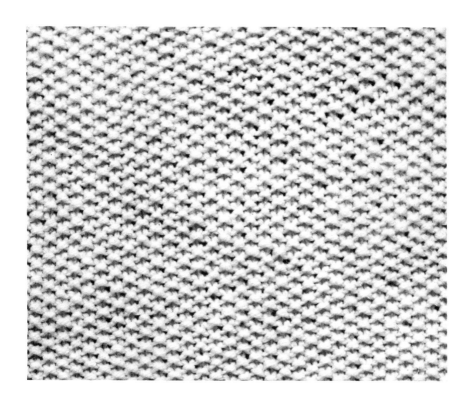

The simplest of the alternating knit and purl pattern stitches, this tiny fabric design has been used variously through the centuries as a foil for the boldly embossed Aran Isle patterns, a background for coats of arms, a solid fill for alternating lacy areas, and by beginners learning to change from a knit to a purl stitch across a row.

Suggested uses: Mufflers, men's wear, place setting mats, socks, slippers, afghan squares, hot mats, caps

Cast on an uneven number of stitches.

Row 1: *K 1, p 1*. Repeat between *'s across row, and end: K 1.
Row 2: Same as Row 1.

DOUBLE MOSS STITCH

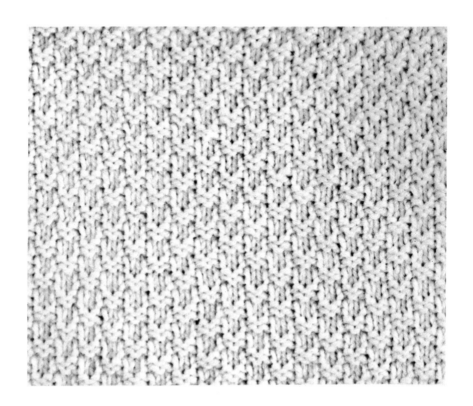

This pattern is exactly what its name indicates, the old favorite Moss Stitch in a double multiple version.

Suggested uses: Alternating afghan squares, men's wear, socks, slippers, mufflers, hot mats, background fabric for bold motifs

Cast on a multiple of 4 stitches.

Row 1: *K 2, p 2*. Repeat between *'s across row.
Row 2: Same as Row 1.
Row 3: *P 2, k 2*. Repeat across row.
Row 4: Same as Row 3.

CHELSEA

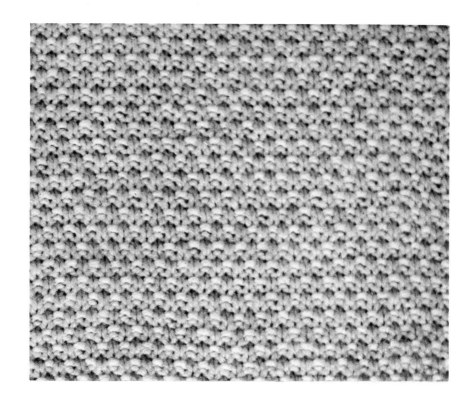

A variation of the Double Moss Stitch, with the stitches being doubled vertically instead of horizontally.

Suggested uses: Background fabric, socks, slippers, men's wear, caps, hot mats, upholstery fabric

Cast on an uneven number of stitches.

Row 1: *K 1, p 1*. Repeat between *'s across row, and end: K 1.
Row 2: *P 1, k 1*. Repeat across row and end: P 1.
Row 3: Same as Row 2.
Row 4: Same as Row 1.

DIAGONAL STITCH

Cast on a multiple of 8 stitches.

Row 1: *K 4, p 4*. Repeat between *'s across row.

Row 2: P 1, *k 4, p 4*. Repeat between *'s across row, and end: K 4, p 3.

Row 3: K 2, *p 4, k 4*. Repeat between *'s across row and end: P 4, k 2.

Row 4: P 3, *k 4, p 4*. Repeat between *'s across row and end: K 4, p 1.

Row 5: *P 4, k 4*. Repeat between *'s across row.

Row 6: K 1, *p 4, k 4*. Repeat between *'s across row and end: P 4, k 3.

Row 7: P 2, *k 4, p 4*. Repeat between *'s across row and end: K 4, p 2.

Row 8: K 3, *p 4, k 4*. Repeat between *'s across row and end: P 4, k 1.

BABY CABLE

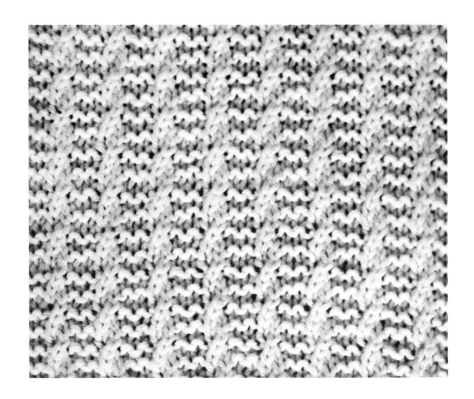

An extremely popular and useful stitch. This small cable twist can be used by itself or inserted between large cables (see Combination Cable, page 34).

Suggested uses: Men's wear, ornamental collars, cuffs, pockets, afghan strips, edges, panels

Cast on a multiple of 4 stitches.

Row 1: P 1, *k 2, p 2*. Repeat between *'s across row and end: K 2, p 1.
Row 2: Purl.
Row 3: P 1, *twist 2, p 2*. Repeat between *'s across row → and end last repeat : Twist 2, p 1.
Row 4: Purl.

CABLE

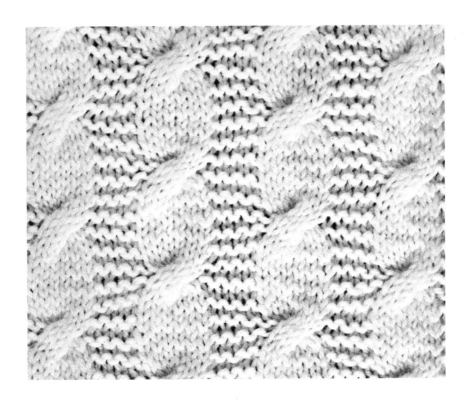

Cast on a multiple of 20 stitches.

Row 1: *P 2, k 6, p 2*. Repeat between *'s across row (taking note that each repeat begins and ends with a p 2).

Row 2 (and all even-numbered rows): Purl.

Row 3: Same as Row 1.

Row 5: *P 2, cable 6 (3 over 3), p 4, k 6, p 2*. Repeat between *'s across row.

Rows 7 and 9: Same as Row 1.

Row 11: *P 2, k 6, p 4, cable 6 (3 over 3), p 2*. Repeat between *'s across row.

Row 12: Purl.

WIDE AND NARROW CABLE

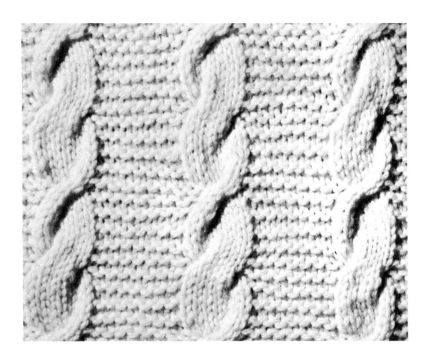

An interesting cable variation that can be used alone or combined with other vertical designs.

Suggested uses: Men's wear, socks, slippers, mufflers, alternating afghan strips, drapery fabric, caps, hats, handbags

Cast on a multiple of 15 stitches.

Row 1: *P 4, k 7, p 4*. Repeat between *'s across row.
Row 2 (and all even-numbered rows): Purl.
Rows 3 and 5: Same as Row 1.
Row 7: *P 4, cable 7 (2 over 5: place 5 sts on cable needle, hold to back of work, k 2, knit sts onto right needle from cable needle), p 4*. Repeat across row.
Rows 9, 11, 13, and 15: Same as Row 1.
Row 17: *P 4, cable 7 (5 over 2: place 2 sts on cable needle, hold to back of work, k 5, knit sts from cable needle), p 4.
Row 19: Same as Row 1.
Row 20: Purl.

COMBINATION CABLE

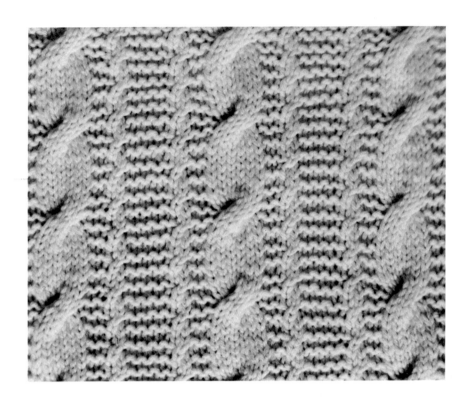

Cast on a multiple of 18 stitches.

Row 1: *P 2, k 2, p 2, k 6, p 2, k 2, p 2*. Repeat between *'s across row.

Row 2 (and all even-numbered rows): Purl.

Row 3: *P 2, twist 2, p 2, k 6, p 2, twist 2, p 2*. Repeat across row.

Row 5: Same as Row 1.

Row 7: Same as Row 3.

Row 9: *P 2, k 2, p 2, cable 6 (3 over 3), p 2, k 2, p 2*. Repeat across row.

Row 11: Same as Row 3.

Row 12: Purl.

HARRISON CABLE

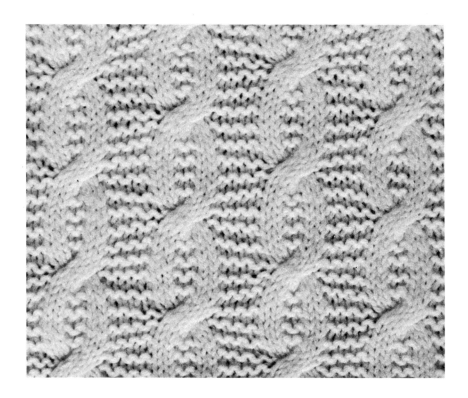

Cast on a multiple of 20 stitches.

Row 1: *P 2, k 2, p 2, k 2, p 4, k 6, p 2*. Repeat between *'s across row (keeping in mind that each repeat begins and ends with a p 2).
Row 2 (and all even-numbered rows): Purl.
Row 3: *P 2, k 2, p 2, k 2, p 4, cable next 6 sts (3 over 3), p 2*. Repeat between *'s across row.
Row 5: *P 2, k 2, p 2, k 2, p 4, k 2, p 2, k 2, p 2*. Repeat between *'s across row.
Row 7: *P 2, k 6, p 4, k 2, p 2, k 2, p 2*. Repeat between *'s across row.
Row 9: *P 2, cable next 6 sts (3 over 3), p 4, k 2, p 2, k 2, p 2*. Repeat between *'s across row.
Row 11: Same as Row 5.
Row 12: Purl.

BOAT-NECK PULLOVER
in Harrison Cable Pattern

Materials required: 6 4-oz skeins 4-ply knitting worsted, 1 pair ⚡7 knitting needles (for ribbing), and 1 pair ⚡9 knitting needles (for body of pullover)

NOTE: It is suggested that materials be purchased at a department store or knit shop employing a knitting instructor so that assistance can be obtained, if necessary, in making the following article. If a larger or smaller size is needed, or another pattern stitch is desired, assistance and directions for these can also be obtained.

Stitch gauge using ⚡9 needles: 1 pattern (20 sts) equal 4¼".

Size 40–42

BACK: Using ⚡7 needles, cast on 100 sts and work in k 1, p 1 ribbing for 4". Change to ⚡9 needles and work in Harrison Cable Pattern until work measures 15" (including ribbing). Bind off 10 sts each side once, then continue working in pattern over these 80 sts until sleeve inset measures 8½" from bound-off sts. Bind off all sts loosely.

FRONT: Work as for back until work measures 7" above bound-off sts of sleeve inset. At beginning of next row, work in pattern across 20 sts, bind off next 40 sts loosely, work in pattern across remaining sts. Working each side separately, continue in pattern until sleeve inset measures 8½" above bound-off sts at underarm. Bind off all sts loosely.

SLEEVE (make 2): Using ⚡7 needles, cast on 46 sts and work in k 1, p 1 ribbing for 4". Change to ⚡9 needles and work in Harrison Cable Pattern over the middle 40 sts, purling the 3 end sts on each side every row.
　　Increase 1 st each side every ½", purling these increase sts, until there are 60 sts on needles, then work in pattern over the entire 60 sts, and at the same time continue increasing 1 st each side every ½" and purling these increase sts, until there are 80 sts on needle. Work in pattern

over all sts on needle, without further increases, until work measures 20″ (or desired sleeve length) from beginning of work, including ribbing. Bind off all sts loosely.

Sew shoulder and side seams. Sew sleeve seams from lower edge to within 2″ of top edge at underarm. Leave this open. Set sleeve into inset by sewing bound-off edge sts to straight edge across shoulder. Sew the 2″ unsewn seam (at top underarm of sleeve) to underarm bound-off sts. The drawing below shows a square-set sleeve.

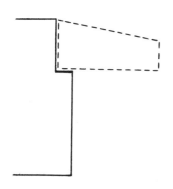

RIBBED COLLAR: Using #7 needles, cast on 156 sts and work in k 1, p 1 ribbing for 6″. Bind off all sts loosely.

Sew narrow edges of ribbed collar together; pin bound-off edge around neckline with seam at center back of neckline. Sew these bound-off sts to neck edge.

Block to exact measurements.

VERTICAL STRIPE

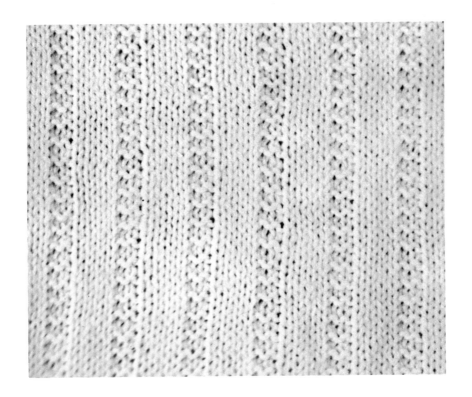

An excellent pattern for the beginner, and very useful as a background stitch.

Suggested uses: Men's wear, socks, slippers, alternating afghan strips, children's wear

Cast on a multiple of 6 stitches plus 2.

Row 1: *P 2, k 4*. Repeat between *'s across row and end: P 2.
Row 2: Purl.

EYELET BAND

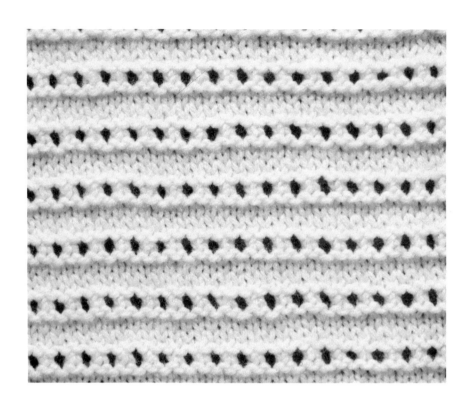

Cast on an odd number of stitches.

Row 1: K 1, *o, k 2 tog*. Repeat between *'s across row.
Rows 2 and 3: Knit.
Row 4: Purl.
Rows 5 and 6: Knit.

MONIQUE

Cast on a multiple of 11 stitches plus 1.

Row 1: K 1, *o, k 3, k 2 tog, k 2 tog, k 3, o, k 1*. Repeat between *'s across row.

Row 2: Knit across row, knitting each over (o) as a separate st.

Row 3: Same as Row 1.

Row 4: Same as Row 2.

Row 5: Knit a triple throw into each st across row.

Row 6: Knit across row, knitting the first strand of each triple throw and dropping second and third strands from left needle without working.

JACQUELINE

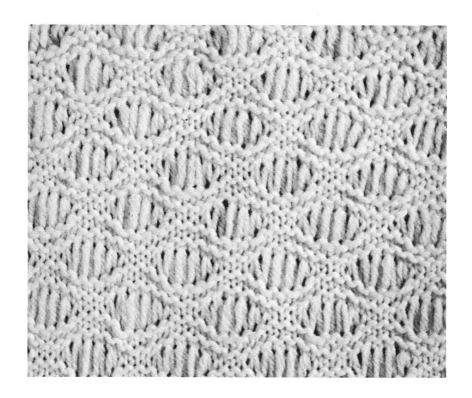

Cast on a multiple of 8 stitches.

Row 1: Knit.
Row 2: Knit.
Row 3: K 2, *knit a triple throw into each of next 4 sts, k 4*. Repeat between *'s across row → and end last repeat: K 2 (instead of k 4).
Row 4: Knit across row, knitting the first strand of each triple throw and dropping second and third strands from left needle without working.
Row 5: Knit.
Row 6: Knit.
Row 7: Knit a triple throw into 2 sts, *k 4, knit a triple throw into next 4 sts*. Repeat between *'s across row → and end last repeat: Knit a triple throw into next 2 sts (instead of into 4).
Row 8: Repeat Row 4.

BOW KNOT

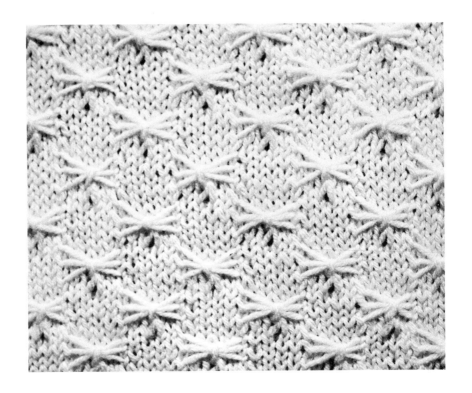

A favorite of the Mid-Victorian period, combining a crisp and simple all-over pattern with a closed fabric that can be used for many items.

Suggested uses: Hats, handbags, scarves, women's wear, alternating afghan squares, ornamental pockets, collars, cuffs

Cast on a multiple of 10 stitches plus 2.

Row 1: K 1, *k 5, sl 5 (purlwise) with yarn in front*. Repeat between *'s across row and end: K 1.
Row 2: Purl.
Row 3: Same as Row 1.
Row 4: Purl.
Row 5: Same as Row 1.
Row 6: P 3, *insert right needle under the 3 strands on front of fabric

and knit as one st, p 1, pass the 3-strand st over the st just purled, p 9*. Repeat between *'s across row → and end last repeat: P 8 (instead of p 9).

Row 7: K 1, *sl 5 (as in Row 1), k 5*. Repeat between *'s and end: K 1.

Row 8: Purl.

Row 9: Same as Row 7.

Row 10: Purl.

Row 11: Same as Row 7.

Row 12: P 8, *work Bow Knot as described in Row 6, p 1, pass bow-knot st over st just purled, p 9*. Repeat between *'s across row → and end last repeat: P 3 (instead of p 9).

KAREN

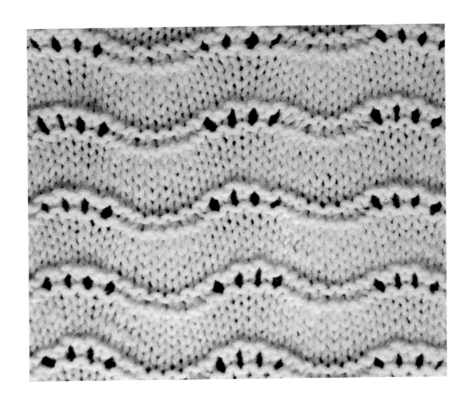

Cast on a multiple of 13 stitches plus 1.

Row 1: *K 1, o, k 1, o, k 1, (k 2 tog) 4 times, k 1, o, k 1, o*.
Repeat between *'s across row and end: K 1.
Row 2: Knit.
Row 3: Knit.
Row 4: Purl.
Row 5: Knit.
Row 6: Purl.
Row 7: Knit.
Row 8: Knit.

II
UNIQUE AND UNUSUAL

BOWS IN ROWS

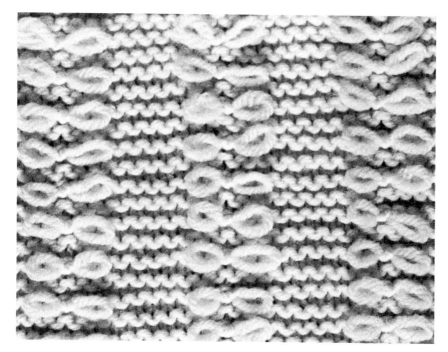

A versatile pattern stitch designed especially for this collection.

Suggested uses: Blouses, shells, cardigans, ornamental collars, cuffs, pockets, panels, edgings, alternating afghan strips, hats, handbags, hot mats, place setting mats, decorator pillows, drapery fabric

Cast on a multiple of 10 stitches plus 1, using ✕10 knitting needles and yarn suitable for ✕10 needles, such as knitting worsted or Germantown.

Row 1: Knit.

Row 2: K 5, *3-throw, k 1, 3-throw, k 9*. Repeat between *'s across row → and end last repeat: K 5 (instead of k 9).

Row 3: K 5, *drop 3-throw from left needle (without working) and to front of fabric, k 1, drop 3-throw, k 9*. Repeat between *'s across row → and end last repeat: K 5 (instead of k 9).

→ **TIE BOWS:** Before working Row 4, insert point of free needle into first pair of loops and pull up snugly to take the slack out of sts between and on either side of these 2 loops. Remove needle from loops and tie this pair of loops tog in a firm square knot. Repeat this procedure across row.

Row 4: Knit.

SHELL in Bows in Rows Pattern

Materials required: 3 4-oz skeins 4-ply knitting worsted, 1 pair ✳10 knitting needles, 1 ✳00 crochet hook.

NOTE: It is suggested that materials be purchased at a department store or knit shop employing a knitting instructor so that assistance can be obtained, if necessary, in making the following article.

Stitch gauge: 4 stitches equal 1″.

>Size 32–34:   Cast on 71 sts.
>Size 36–38:   Cast on 81 sts.

BACK AND FRONT are identical. Make 2 of the following: Work in Bows in Rows Pattern until fabric measures 14″ from beginning (or desired length from lower edge to underarm). Shape arm opening: At beginning of next 2 rows bind off 8 sts, then k 2 tog at beginning of next 4 rows. Continue in pattern over remaining sts until arm opening measures:

>5″ for size 34–36
>5½″ for size 38–40

and shape neckline as follows: With reverse side facing work in pattern across 11 sts, then bind off sts across row until 11 sts remain (10 sts on left needle, 1 st on right needle) and work in pattern to end of row. Working each shoulder separately, continue in pattern until arm opening measures:

7″ for size 34–36
7½″ for size 38–40

and bind off all sts loosely.

ASSEMBLING AND FINISHING: Sew side and shoulder seams. Work 2 rows of single crochet around neckline and arm openings. Block to exact measurements.

CHECKERBOARD BOWS

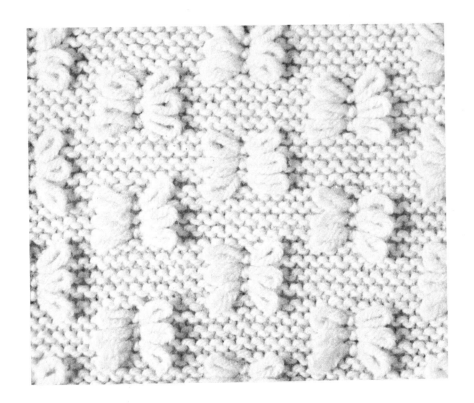

One of the new Montage designs, formulated especially for this collection. This pattern seems to have a sort of gaiety and flair all its own.

Suggested uses: Afghans, scatter rugs, coverlets, ornamental insertions and edgings, hot mats, decorator pillows

Cast on a multiple of 16 stitches plus 9, using ✸10 knitting needles and 4-ply knitting worsted or equivalent.

Row 1: Knit.
Row 2: K 4, *3-throw, k 1, 3-throw, k 15*. Repeat between *'s across row → and end last repeat: K 4 (instead of k 15).
Row 3: K 4, *drop 3-throw, k 1, drop 3-throw, k 15*. Repeat between *'s across row → and end last repeat: K 4 (instead of k 15).
→ **TIE BOWS:** Insert point of free needle into each pair of loops and pull up snugly to take the slack out of sts between and on either side of these 2 loops. Tie each pair of loops tog in a firm square knot.

Row 4: Same as Row 2.

Row 5: Same as Row 3.

Row 6: Same as Row 2.

Row 7: Same as Row 3.

Row 8: Knit.

Row 9: Knit.

Row 10: K 12, *3-throw, k 1, 3-throw, k 15*. Repeat between *'s across row → and end last repeat: K 12 (instead of k 15).

Row 11: K 12, *drop 3-throw, k 1, drop 3-throw, k 15*. Repeat between *'s across row → and end last repeat: K 12 (instead of k 15). Tie loops, as in Row 3.

Row 12: Same as Row 10.

Row 13: Same as Row 11.

Row 14: Same as Row 10.

Row 15: Same as Row 11.

Row 16: Knit.

FRILLS AND PEARLS

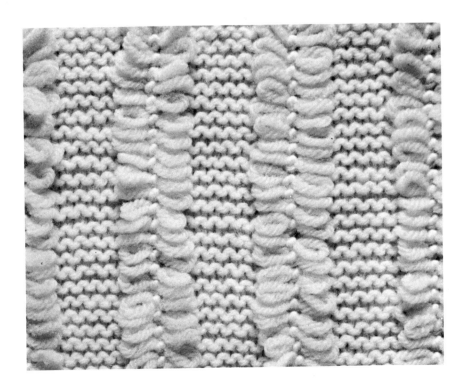

Another of the Montage designs, this fabric is interesting to knit, simple to do, and a conversation piece wherever it is used.

Suggested uses: Alternating afghan strips, ornamental pockets, cuffs, collars, edgings, scatter rugs, hot mats, hats, handbags, decorator pillows

Cast on a multiple of 11 stitches for every vertical row of pattern desired, using ⚹10 knitting needles and 4-ply knitting worsted or equivalent.

Knit across 1 row before beginning pattern (on the first row only; do not repeat).

Row 1: *K 5, 3-throw, k 1, 3-throw, k 5*. Repeat between *'s.

Row 2: *K 5, drop 3-throw, k 1, drop 3-throw, k 5*. Repeat between *'s.

→ **TIE BOWS:** Insert point of free needle into each pair of loops and pull up snugly to take slack out of sts between and on either side of these 2 loops. Remove needle from loops and tie each pair of loops tog in a firm square knot.

DECORATOR PILLOW
in Checkerboard Bows Pattern

Materials required: 2 4-oz skeins 4-ply knitting worsted, 1 pair #10 knitting needles, 1 #00 crochet hook, ⅔ yard Iron-On Pellon (obtainable at yardage and department stores), approximately 4 oz shredded polyester foam for stuffing (obtainable at hobby shops and variety stores)

Approximate size: 11½″×13″

FRONT: Cast on 57 sts and work in Checkerboard Bows Pattern until fabric measures 11½″ from beginning. Bind off all sts knitwise on reverse side loosely.

BACK: Cast on 57 sts and work in Garter Stitch until fabric measures 11½″ from beginning. Bind off all sts knitwise loosely.

FINISHING: Work 1 row of single crochet around edges of each piece, working 3 single crochet sts in each corner. Block front and back pieces to exactly 11½″×13″. Cut 2 pieces of Iron-On Pellon exactly 11¼″×12¾″ and bond a square of Pellon to back of each pillow piece, allowing crocheted edge to extend ¼″ beyond Pellon backing on all sides. Place pieces tog, right side out, and crochet these 2 edges tog, working 3 single crochet sts in each corner, and leaving a 6″ opening on one edge. Fill pillow through this opening with shredded polyester foam, being sure to pack corners well. Crochet edges of opening tog and fasten yarn securely.

DECORATOR PILLOW
in Frills and Pearls Pattern

Materials required: 2 4-oz skeins 4-ply knitting worsted, 1 pair ✕10 knitting needles, 1 ✕ 00 crochet hook, ⅔ yard Iron-On Pellon (obtainable at yardage and department stores), approximately 4 oz shredded polyester foam for stuffing (obtainable at hobby shops and variety stores)

Approximate size: 9½″✕13″

FRONT: Cast on 66 sts and work in Frills and Pearls Pattern until fabric measures 9½″ from beginning. Bind off all sts knitwise on reverse side loosely.

BACK: Cast on 66 sts and work in Garter Stitch until fabric measures 9½″ from beginning. Bind off all sts knitwise loosely.

FINISHING: Work 1 row of single crochet around edges of each piece, working 3 single crochet sts in each corner. Block front and back pieces to exactly 9½″✕13″. If a substitute pattern is used, see NOTE below before proceeding. Cut 2 pieces of Iron-On Pellon exactly 9¼″✕12¾″ (or ¼″ less than actual size of knitted fabric around all edges if size varies from 9½✕13″). Bond a square of Pellon to back of each pillow piece, allowing crocheted edge to extend ¼″ beyond the Pellon backing on all sides. Place pieces together, right side out, and crochet edges together, working 3 single crochets in each corner, and leaving a 6″ opening on one edge. Fill pillow through this opening with the shredded polyester foam, being sure to pack corners well. Crochet edges of opening together and fasten yarn securely.

NOTE: If size of pillow pieces varies from specified dimensions, lay the front pillow piece on a firm surface, smooth out fabric as much as possible, and measure carefully. These dimensions should be used when blocking.

RIBBONS AND BOWS

One of the Montage designs, this pattern has a myriad of uses with its closed fabric combined with an interesting yet simple design.

Suggested uses: Afghan strips, women's wear, coverlets, decorator pillows, hats, handbags, ornamental collars, cuffs, pockets, panels

Cast on a multiple of 20 sts, using ✕10 knitting needles and 4-ply knitting worsted or equivalent.

Row 1: P 3, *k 4, p 6*. Repeat between *'s across row → and end last repeat: P 3 (instead of p 6).

Row 2: Purl.

Row 3: Same as Row 1.

Row 4: P 3, *2-throw, p 4, 2-throw, p 16*. Repeat between *'s across row → and end last repeat: P 13 (instead of p 16).

Row 5: P 3, *k 4, p 6, drop 2-throw to front of work, k 4, drop 2-throw to front of work, p 6*. Repeat between *'s across row → and end last repeat: P 3 (instead of p 6).

→ **TIE BOWS:** Insert point of free needle into each pair of loops and pull up snugly to take slack out of sts between and on either side of these loops. Remove needle from loops and tie each pair of loops together in a firm square knot. (See pattern stitch photo.)

Row 6: Purl.

Row 7: Same as Row 1.

Row 8: Purl.

Row 9: Same as Row 1.

Row 10: P 13, *2-throw, p 4, 2-throw, p 16*. Repeat between *'s across row → and end last repeat: P 3 (instead of p 16).

Row 11: P 3, *drop 2-throw to front of work, k 4, drop 2-throw to front of work, p 6, k 4, p 6*. Repeat between *'s across row → and end last repeat: P 3 (instead of p 6). → Tie bows, as before.

Row 12: Purl.

VIOLET

A Montage fabric designed especially for this collection. Use it with mauve, orchid, bright violet, or purple tones.

Suggested uses: Ornamental trim, edgings, collars, cuffs, pockets, panels, hats, handbags, decorator pillows

Cast on a multiple of 10 stitches plus 1, using ╳10 knitting needles and suitable yarn, such as knitting worsted, Germantown, or other similar weight material. A size G crochet hook is required for this pattern.

Knit across 3 rows before beginning pattern (once only; do not repeat).
Violet Row 1 (reverse side): K 5, *4-throw, k 1, 4-throw, k 9*. Repeat between *'s across row → and end last repeat: K 5 (instead of k 9).
Violet Row 2: Knit across row, slipping all 4-throw loops from left needle and to front of work (without knitting), → then insert free needle into each pair of loops (1 pair at a time) and pull up snugly, holding thumb and forefinger of left hand at base of loops, to take slack out of sts between

and on either side of pair of loops. → Tie each pair of loops in a single knot. → Repeat Violet Rows 1 and 2 (once more only).

Violet Row 3: K 5, *3-throw, k 1, 3-throw, k 9*. Repeat between *'s across row and end last repeat: K 5 (instead of k 9).

Violet Row 4: Same as Violet Row 2; → pull up loops but do not tie. → Tie loops to form violets as follows: Insert crochet hook into first 2 pairs of loops made, then place crochet hook in a horizontal position over knitting needle so that all 4 of these loops lie between 3-throw loops and are held flat by crochet hook. Pick up last-made pair of loops and tie in firm square knot over both pairs of previously made loops. See illustration of this pattern stitch, noting positions of each pair of loops in each violet. Remove crochet hook and tie each group in this manner across row.

→ Knit across next 8 rows. This will make 4 purl ridges on right side of fabric between violet rows. Complete last row on right side of fabric.

Violet Row 5: K 10, *4-throw, k 1, 4-throw, k 9*. Repeat between *'s across row and end: K 1.

Violet Row 6: Same as Violet Row 2.

→ Repeat Violet Rows 5 and 6 (once more only).

Violet Row 7: K 10, *3-throw, k 1, 3-throw, k 9*. Repeat between *'s across row and end: K 1.

Violet Row 8: Same as Violet Row 2; pull up loops but do not tie. → Tie loops to form violets, as before.

→ Knit across next 8 rows, as before.

Repeat from Violet Row 1 for pattern.

SHORT-SLEEVE BLOUSE in Violet Pattern

Materials required: 3 4-oz skeins 4-ply knitting worsted, 1 pair ⚓10 knitting needles, 1 ⚓G crochet hook

NOTE: It is suggested that materials be purchased at a department store or knit shop employing a knitting instructor so that assistance can be obtained, if necessary, in making the following article. If a larger or smaller size is needed, or another pattern stitch is desired, assistance and directions for these can also be obtained.

Stitch gauge: 4 stitches equal 1".

Cast on 71 sts for size 32–34. Cast on 81 sts for size 36–38.

FRONT: Work in Violet Pattern Stitch until there are 23 purl ridges and 3 rows of violets on front of fabric, then work in Stockinette Stitch (knit front of fabric and purl reverse side) until fabric measures 14" (or desired length to underarm) from beginning of work.

SHAPE SLEEVES: At beginning of next 2 rows, cast on 10 sts (once each side) and again work in Violet Pattern Stitch until 3 rows of violets and 22 purl ridges have been made on front of fabric. Next row: With reverse side facing, work across (26 sts for size 32–34) or (31 sts for size 36–38), then bind off next 39 sts and work across remaining sts (neckline made). Working each shoulder separately, work in Garter Stitch (knit every row) until 4 purl ridges have been made above neckline. Bind off loosely on reverse side. Attach yarn to neckline side of right shoulder and complete in the same way.

BACK: Cast on exact number of sts as for front. Work in Garter Stitch until there are 23 purl ridges on one side. Then work in Stockinette Stitch for exactly the same length as for front. Shape sleeves: Cast on 10 sts at beginning of next 2 rows (once each side) and work once more in Garter Stitch until there are 26 purl ridges from beginning of sleeve. Bind off loosely on reverse side.

Sew shoulder seams on reverse side in whip stitch, catching only the lower loop of bind-off sts on each edge. Sew side seams in flat stitch on right side or in a seam on reverse side. Block to exact measurements.

DAISY

Another Montage pattern designed especially for this collection. The daisies are knitted right into the fabric along with the Garter Stitch background.

Suggested uses: Women's wear, lounge wear, afghan squares, ornamental collars, cuffs, pockets, panels, edgings, decorative mats, winter stoles, hats, handbags, tote bags, decorator pillows, small-window draperies

Cast on a multiple of 10 stitches plus 1. It is suggested that the knitter use ✗10 knitting needles to work this pattern so that the daisy loops (petals) will be of the proper length.

→ Knit across 7 rows before beginning pattern.

Daisy Row 1 (reverse side of fabric): K 5, *4-throw, k 1, 4-throw, k 9*. Repeat between *'s across row → and end last repeat: K 5 (instead of k 9).

Daisy Row 2: Knit across row, slipping all 4-throw loops from left needle and to front of work without knitting, → then insert free needle into each pair of loops (one pair at a time) and pull up snugly, holding thumb and forefinger of left hand at base of loops, to take the slack out of sts between and on either side of this pair of loops. Tie each pair of loops into a single knot.

→ Repeat Daisy Rows 1 and 2, pull up loops → but do not tie.

→ Repeat Daisy Rows 1 and 2 once more, pull up loops, and again tie these in a single knot. (This will make a total of 3 pairs of loops in a vertical line in each motif across row.)

→ Tie loops to form daisies as follows: Tie upper right loop and lower left loop into a single knot. Tie upper left loop and lower right loop into a single knot. Tie middle pair of loops into a firm square knot across the 2 single knots just tied. Tie each group (3 pairs of loops) in this manner across row. See photo of pattern.

→ Knit across next 12 rows. This will make 6 purl ridges on right side of fabric between daisy rows. Complete last row on right side of fabric.

Daisy Row 3 (reverse side): K 10, *4-throw, k 1, 4-throw, k 9*. Repeat between *'s across row and end: K 1.

Daisy Row 4: Same as Daisy Row 2.

→ Repeat Daisy Rows 3 and 4, pull up loops → but do not tie.

→ Repeat Daisy Rows 3 and 4 once more, pull up loops and tie in a single knot. (This will make a total of 3 pairs of loops in each motif across row, as before.)

→ Tie loops to form daisies as before.

→ Knit across 12 rows, as before.

Repeat from Daisy Row 1 for pattern.

SHELL in Daisy Pattern

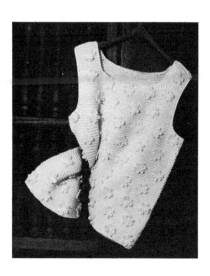

Materials required: 3 4-oz skeins 4-ply knitting worsted, 1 pair ✕10 knitting needles, 1 ✕00 crochet hook. Using the same general directions as for Shell in Bows in Rows on page 48, work in Daisy Pattern for front of shell, and back in Garter Stitch.

DRAGONFLY BORDER

Cast on a multiple of 10 stitches plus 1, using ⚹10 knitting needles and 4-ply knitting worsted or equivalent.

→ Knit across 3 rows.

Dragonfly Row 1 (reverse side): K 5, *5-throw, k 1, 5-throw, k 9*. Repeat between *'s across row → and end last repeat: K 5 (instead of k 9).

Dragonfly Row 2: Knit across row, slipping all 5-throw loops from left needle and to front (without working) → then insert free needle into each pair of loops (1 pair at a time) and pull up snugly, holding thumb and forefinger of left hand at base of loops, to take slack out of sts between and on either side of pair of loops, then tie each pair of loops into a firm square knot.

→ Knit across next 6 rows.

Dragonfly Row 3 (reverse side): K 5, *3-throw, k 1, 3-throw, k 9*. Repeat between *'s across row → and end last repeat: K 5 (instead of k 9).

Dragonfly Row 4: Knit across row, slipping all 3-throw loops from left needle, and pulling up snugly with free needle (as in Row 2) → then, before tying, separate each pair of loops and lay 5-throw loops across, then tie these 3-throw loops across in a firm square knot; see photo of Dragonfly Border (body of dragonfly and lower wings).

Dragonfly Row 5 (reverse side): K 5, *4-throw, k 1, 4-throw, k 9*. Repeat between *'s across row → and end last repeat: K 5 (instead of k 9).

Dragonfly Row 6: Knit across row, slipping all 4-throw loops from left needle and pulling up snugly (as in Row 2) → then, before tying, separate each pair of loops, lay upper body of dragonfly across these and tie this last pair of loops across body in a firm square knot, as in photo.

→ Knit across next 5 rows to complete border.

SPRING POSY BORDER

Cast on a multiple of 10 stitches plus 1, using ✳10 knitting needles and 4-ply knitting worsted or similar. A size G crochet hook is required for this pattern.

→ Knit across 5 rows.

Spring Posy Row 1 (reverse side): K 5, *5-throw, k 1, 5-throw, k 9*. Repeat between *'s across row → and end last repeat: K 5 (instead of k 9).

Spring Posy Row 2: Knit across row, slipping all 5-throw loops from left needle and to front (without working) → then insert free needle into each pairs of loops (1 pair at a time) and pull up snugly, holding thumb and forefinger of left hand at base of loops, to take slack out of sts between and on either side of pair of loops; then tie each pair of loops in a firm square knot.

Spring Posy Row 3: Same as Row 1.

Spring Posy Row 4: Same as Row 2.

Spring Posy Row 5 (reverse side): K 5, *4-throw, k 1, 4-throw, k 9*. Repeat between *'s across row → and end last repeat: K 5 (instead of k 9).

Spring Posy Row 6: Same as Row 2.

Spring Posy Row 7 (reverse side): K 5, 3-throw, k 1, 3-throw, k 9*. Repeat between *'s across row → and end last repeat: K 5 (instead of k 9).

Spring Posy Row 8: Knit across row, slipping all 3-throws from left needle and pulling up snugly (as in Row 2) → then, before tying, insert crochet hook into the first 3 pairs of loops made and place crochet hook over needle so that all 6 of these loops lie between the pair of 3-throw loops just made and are held flat by crochet hook. Pick up last-made pair of loops (3-throws) and tie in a firm square knot over all 3 pairs of previously made loops. (See photo.) Remove crochet hook and tie each group across row.

→ Knit across next 9 rows to complete border.

BRIDGET

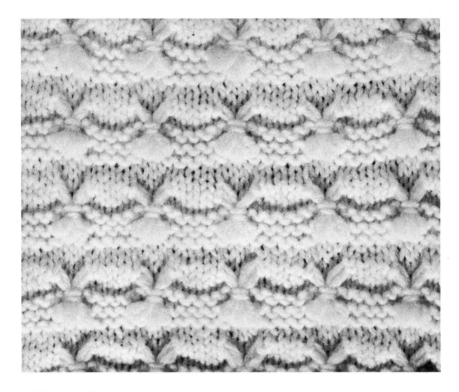

This pert little pattern can be used in many ways when the knitter is looking for something different. It is a conversation piece however it is used.

Suggested uses: Hats, caps, handbags, tote bags, decorator pillows, shells, ornamental collars, cuffs, pockets, panels, edgings

Cast on a multiple of 7 stitches plus 4. A ✖0 or larger crochet hook is required for this pattern.

ROWS 1, 2, 3, 4, and 5: Knit.
ROW 6: Purl.
ROW 7: Knit.
ROW 8: Purl.
ROW 9: Knit.
ROW 10: Purl.
ROW 11: *K 4, unravel the next 3 sts down 3 rows; with right needle pick up these 3 sts in back of strands and place them on left needle, knit these 3 sts*. Repeat between *'s across row and end: K 4.

66

→ When Row 11 is completed, insert crochet hook up through the 2 purl sts directly below central st (between strands) and pull strands down through these purl sts, as in illustration.

ROW 12: Knit.

NOTE: If item made from above pattern stitch is to have vigorous usage, tack loops, using matching yarn and overcast stitch, firmly at back, directly behind the purl stitches through which loops have been pulled.

LANTERN

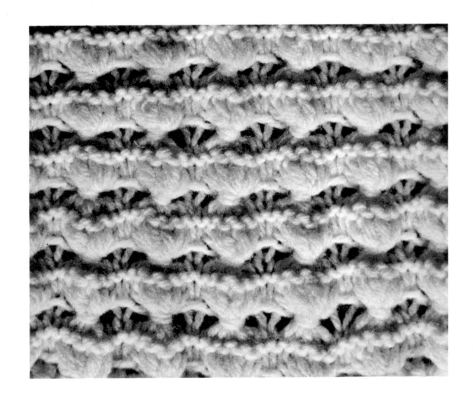

Cast on a multiple of 6 stitches plus 1.

Row 1: *K 1, knit a triple throw into next 5 sts*. Repeat between *'s and end: K 1.

Row 2: *K 1, slip-cluster next 5 sts*. Repeat between *'s and end: K 1.

Row 3 (right side of work): Knit, knitting each st in each slip-cluster.

Row 4: Knit.

ANDREA

Cast on a multiple of 10 stitches plus 2.

Row 1: Knit.

Row 2: Knit.

Row 3: K 1, *k 5, knit a triple throw into next 5 sts*. Repeat between *'s across row and end: K 1.

Row 4: K 1, *slip-cluster next 5 sts, k 5*. Repeat between *'s across row and end: K 1.

Row 5: Knit.

Row 6: Knit.

Row 7: K 1, *knit a triple throw into next 5 sts, k 5*. Repeat between *'s across row and end: K 1.

Row 8: K 6, *slip-cluster next 5 sts, k 5*. Repeat between *'s across row → and end last repeat: K 1 (instead of k 5).

69

LACY DAISY

A pattern of delicate and lacy appearance, this can be used in many interesting ways where a moderately lacy all-over pattern is required.

Suggested uses: Blouses, dresses, stoles, cardigans, coverlets, baby items, place setting mats, tablecloths, lounge wear, ornamental collars, cuffs, pockets, hats, handbags

Cast on a multiple of 6 stitches plus 1.

Row 1 (reverse side of fabric): Knit.

Row 2: K 1, *knit a triple throw into next 5 sts, k 1*. Repeat between *'s across row.

Row 3: K 1, *slip-cluster next 5 sts, k 1*. Repeat between *'s across row.

Row 4: Knit, knitting each st in each slip-cluster.

Row 5: Knit.

Row 6: K 4, *knit a triple throw into next 5 sts, k 1*. Repeat between *'s across row and end: K 3.

Row 7: K 4, *slip-cluster next 5 sts, k 1*. Repeat between *'s across row and end: K 3.

Row 8: Same as Row 4.

PAINTED DAISY

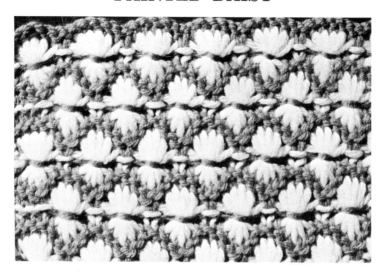

A 2-color version of Lacy Daisy that is especially attractive when used in interior décor and household items. Contrasting colors, in approximately the same amounts, are needed: one white or very light and the other, to outline the daisy, should be a color of high contrast.

Suggested uses: Drapery and upholstery fabric, place setting mats, afghans, coverlets, bedspreads, baby items, hot mats, decorative centerpieces, stoles

Using contrasting color, with which to outline each daisy, cast on a multiple of 6 stitches plus 1.

Row 1: Knit across row; break contrasting color yarn and attach main color.

Row 2: K 1, *knit a triple throw into next 5 sts, k 1*. Repeat between *'s across row; break main color and attach contrasting color.

Row 3: K 1, *slip-cluster next 5 sts, k 1*. Repeat between *'s across row.

Row 4: Knit, knitting each st in each slip-cluster.

Row 5: Knit across row; break contrasting color and attach main color.

Row 6: K 4, *knit a triple throw into next 5 sts, k 1*. Repeat between *'s across row and end: K 3; break main color and attach contrasting color.

Row 7: K 4, *slip-cluster next 5 sts, k 1*. Repeat between *'s across row and end: K 3.

Row 8: Knit, as in Row 4. Do not break contrasting color; repeat from Row 1.

DAISY CHAIN

An attractive combination of Daisy and Stockinette, designed especially for this collection. This pattern has a remarkable versatility; it can be used upside down or sideways.

Suggested uses: Women's wear, stoles, lounge wear, tablecloths, place setting mats, decorative centerpieces, coverlets, hats, handbags, drapery and upholstery fabric

Cast on a multiple of 6 stitches plus 1.

Row 1: Knit.
Row 2: Purl.
Row 3: Knit.
Row 4 (reverse side): Knit.
Row 5: K 1, *knit a triple throw into next 5 sts, k 1*. Repeat between *'s across row.
Row 6: K 1, *slip-cluster next 5 sts, k 1*. Repeat between *'s across row.

Row 7: Knit, knitting each st in each slip-cluster.

Rows 8 and 9: Knit.

Row 10: Purl.

Rows 11 and 12: Knit.

Row 13: K 4, *knit a triple throw into next 5 sts, k 1*. Repeat between *'s across row and end: K 3.

Row 14: K 4, *slip-cluster 5, k 1*. Repeat between *'s across row and end: K 3.

Rows 15 and 16: Knit.

SHORT-SLEEVE BLOUSE
in Daisy Chain Pattern

Materials required: 3 4-oz skeins 4-ply knitting worsted, 1 pair ✕10 knitting needles

Stitch gauge: 2 Daisy Patterns (12 sts) equal 2¾″.

Cast on 79 sts for size 32–34 (bust measurement).
Cast on 91 sts for size 36–38 (bust measurement).
Cast on 97 sts for size 40–42 (bust measurement).

BACK: Knit across 4 rows, then work in Daisy Chain Pattern, repeating Rows 1 through 16 until fabric measures 13″. (Work should be measured lying flat on firm surface and smoothed out as much as possible.)

SHAPE SLEEVES: At beginning of next 2 rows (once each side) cast on 6 sts (this can be done on any row EXCEPT Rows 6 or 14 of pattern) and continue in pattern until sleeves measure:

5¾″ for size 32–34
6½″ for size 36–38
6¾″ for size 40–42

Then continue in pattern until next slip-cluster row has been completed. Knit across next 5 rows and bind off all sts loosely (knitwise) on reverse side.

FRONT: Cast on same number of sts as for back and knit across 4 rows. Work Rows 9 through 16 of Daisy Chain Pattern, then continue in pattern (repeating Rows 1 through 16). Work as for back to completion.

SLEEVE EDGING: Sew shoulder seams, leaving a 10″ opening for neckline. With right side of fabric facing, pick up sts along the entire edge of sleeve as follows.

46 sts for size 32–34
50 sts for size 36–38
54 sts for size 40–42

inserting needle through edge st loops. Work in Garter Stitch (knit every row) for 4 rows, then bind off all sts (knitwise) very loosely on reverse side. Repeat on corresponding sleeve. Sew up side seams. Block to exact measurements.

TREVA

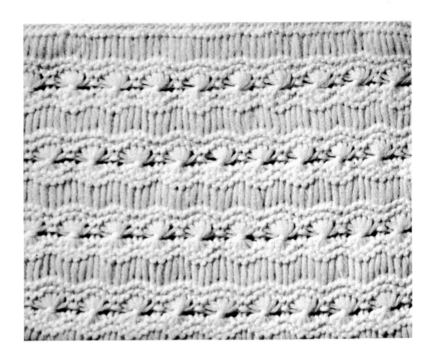

A remarkably beautiful pattern combining Daisy and the triple throw stitch, especially useful when a wide expanse of loosely knitted fabric is needed.

Suggested uses: Scarves, stoles, shrugs, bedjackets, coverlets, drapery fabric, tablecloths, place setting mats, blouses, women's summer wear

Cast on a multiple of 6 stitches plus 1.

Rows 1 and 2: Knit.
Row 3: K 1, *knit a triple throw into next 5 sts, k 1*. Repeat between *'s across row.
Row 4: K 1, *slip-cluster next 5 sts, k 1*. Repeat between *'s across row.
Row 5: Knit, knitting each st in each slip-cluster.
Rows 6, 7, and 8: Knit.
Row 9: Knit a double throw into first st, then knit a triple throw into each st across row.

76

Row 10: Knit, knitting first strand of each st and slipping second and third strands from left needle without working.

Rows 11 and 12: Knit.

Row 13: K 4, *knit a triple throw into next 5 sts, k 1*. Repeat between *'s across row and end: K 3.

Row 14: K 4, *slip-cluster next 5 sts, k 1*. Repeat between *'s across row and end: K 3.

Row 15: Same as Row 5.

Rows 16, 17, and 18: Knit.

Row 19: Same as Row 9.

Row 20: Same as Row 10.

BABY SHELL

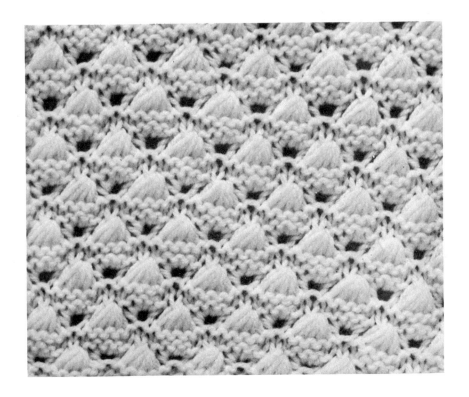

This is the smallest of the shell motifs and resembles the crocheted shell pattern. It is dainty enough for even the smallest of knitted items, yet attractive and interesting in items requiring a large expanse of fabric.

Suggested uses: Baby items, children's wear, women's wear, afghans, upholstery fabric, lounge wear, hats, handbags, mufflers

Cast on a multiple of 6 stitches plus 2.

Row 1: Knit.
Row 2: Knit.
Row 3: K 1, *(k 1, p 1, k 1, p 1, k 1) in next st before slipping it from left needle, knit a double throw into each of next 5 sts* Repeat between *'s across row and end: K 1.
Row 4: K 1, *yarn forward, sl 5 purlwise (slip first strand, drop second strand), slip these 5 long sts back onto left needle and purl them together, k 5*. Repeat between *'s across row and end: K 1.

Row 5: Knit.

Row 6: Knit.

Row 7: K 1, *knit a double throw into each of next 5 sts, (k 1, p 1, k 1, p 1, k 1) into next st*. Repeat between *'s across row and end: K 1.

Row 8: K 6, *yarn forward, sl 5 purlwise and purl tog (as in Row 4), k 5*. Repeat between *'s across row and end: Sl 5 and purl these tog, k 1.

LACY SHELL

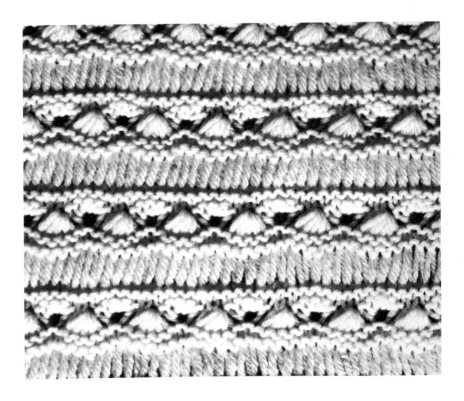

A delicate-looking pattern that knits up quickly and keeps its fragile appearance even in the heavier yarns.

Suggested uses: Stoles, scarves, coverlets, shells, lounge wear, bed jackets, dresses, and blouses

Cast on a multiple of 6 stitches plus 2.

Rows 1 and 2: Knit.
Row 3: K 1, *(k 1, p 1, k 1, p 1, k 1) into next st, knit a double throw into each of next 5 sts*. Repeat between *'s across row and end: K 1.
Row 4: K 1, *yarn forward, sl 5 purlwise (slip first strand, drop second strand), slip these 5 sts back onto left needle and purl them together, k 5*. Repeat between *'s across row and end: K 1.
Rows 5 and 6: Knit.
Row 7: Knit a double throw into first st, then knit a triple throw into each st across row.

Row 8: Knit, knitting the first strand of each st and dropping the second and third strands from left needle without working.

Rows 9 and 10: Knit.

Row 11: K 1, *knit a double throw into each of next 5 sts, (k 1, p 1, k 1, p 1, k 1) into next st*. Repeat between *'s across row and end: K 1.

Row 12: K 6, *yarn forward, sl 5 purlwise and purl these tog (as in Row 4), k 5*. Repeat between *'s across row and end: Sl 5 and purl tog, k 1.

Rows 13 and 14: Knit.

Row 15: Same as Row 7.

Row 16: Same as Row 8.

FRILLY SHELL

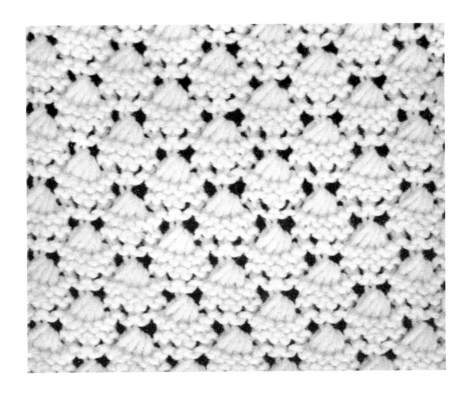

A delicate yet utilitarian pattern with alternating shell motifs that knit up quickly.

Suggested uses: Women's wear, baby wear, stoles, scarves, slipper tops, ornamental collars, cuffs, pockets

Cast on a multiple of 6 stitches plus 1.

Row 1: *K 1, o, k 5, o*. Repeat between *'s across row and end: K 1.
Row 2: Knit.
Row 3: *K 1, o, k 1, knit a double throw into next 5 sts, k 1, o*. Repeat between *'s across row and end: K 1.
Row 4: K 3, *slip 5 (insert needle into first strand without working, slip second strand from left needle, creating a long st) onto right needle, slip these 5 sts back onto left needle and purl all of them tog as 1 st, k 5*. Repeat between *'s across row → and end last repeat: K 3 (instead of k 5).

Row 5: K 3, *o, k 1, o, k 5*. Repeat between *'s across row → and end last repeat: K 3 (instead of k 5).

Row 6: Knit.

Row 7: Knit a double throw into first 3 sts, *k 1, o, k 1, o, k 1, knit a double throw into next 5 sts*. Repeat between *'s across row → and end last repeat: Knit a double throw into last 3 sts (instead of 5 sts).

Row 8: Sl 3, sl back to left needle and purl tog, *k 5, sl 5, return to left needle and purl tog*. Repeat between *'s across row → and end last repeat: Sl 3 (instead of sl 5), slip back onto left needle, and purl tog.

SCALLOPED SHELL

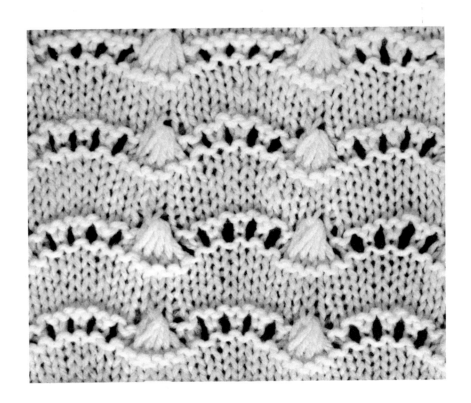

Cast on a multiple of 10 stitches plus 1.

Row 1: *K 1, (o, k 1) twice, knit a double throw into next 5 sts, (k 1, o) twice*. Repeat between *'s across row and end: K 1.

Row 2: *K 5, yarn forward, sl 5 purlwise, (slip first strand of double throw, drop second), yarn to back, k 4*. Repeat between *'s across row and end: K 1.

Row 3: *K 5, sl 5 purlwise, keeping yarn to back, k 4*. Repeat between *'s across row and end: K 1.

Row 4: *P 5, p 5 tog, p 4*. Repeat between *'s across row and end: K 1.

Row 5: Knit.

Row 6: Purl.

Row 7: Knit.

Row 8: Knit.

TOTE BAG in Scalloped Shell Pattern

Materials required: 1 4-oz skein 4-ply knitting worsted, 1 pair ⋕8 knitting needles and 1 pair ⋕7 knitting needles, one round plastic or cardboard bucket-shaped container measuring approximately 7¾" across top and standing 6" high (size can vary slightly). These cardboard or plastic containers can be obtained in paint or hardware stores.

Stitch gauge: ⋕8 needles, 4½ sts equal 1".

Using ⋕8 needles and starting at top edge, cast on 101 sts. Work in Scalloped Shell Pattern Stitch until fabric measures 10". Change to ⋕7 needles and work in k 1, p 1 ribbing for 2¼". Bind off as follows: K 1, *k 2 tog, bind off 1 st*. Repeat between *'s across bind-off row; fasten off last st and break yarn 14" from fabric. Thread this strand through a yarn needle and sew side edges together. Make 2 twisted cords 1 yd in length and starting at seam side, run cord in and out of eyelets at upper edge and tie the 2 ends of cord together in a single knot about 2" below end knots. Starting at opposite side from seam, run the second cord through eyelets and tie ends in single knot as for first cord. Slip round container into bag and draw cords tog to close top. Bag can be thoroughly wet, then rolled in terry-cloth towel until damp dry, then dried over container. This gives the fabric a smooth, blocked appearance.

EMBOSSED SHELL

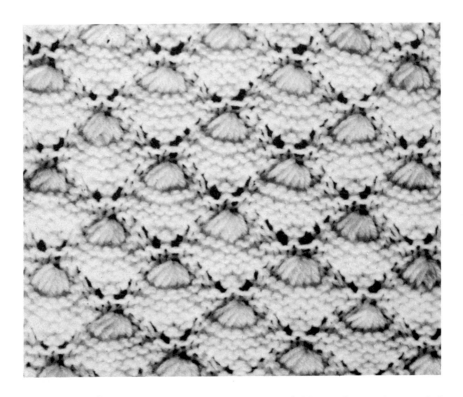

This dramatic shell motif knits up very quickly and can be used in many ways with stunning effect.

Suggested uses: Women's fall and winter wear, carriage covers, stoles, lounge wear, hats, handbags, ornamental collars, cuffs, pockets, panels, edgings

Cast on a multiple of 10 stitches plus 1.

Rows 1 and 2: Knit.
Row 3: K 1, *o, k 9, o, k 1*. Repeat between *'s across row.
Row 4: K 2, *o, k 9, o, k 3*. Repeat between *'s across row → and end last repeat: K 2 (instead of k 3).
Row 5: K 3, *o, k 1, knit a double throw into next 7 sts, k 1, o, k 5*. Repeat between *'s across row and → end last repeat: K 3 (instead of k 5).
Row 6: K 5, *slip next 7 sts onto right needle without working (insert needle purl vise into first strand and slip onto right needle, dropping second

strand) → then slip all 7 of these slipped sts back onto left needle and purl them all together, k 9*. Repeat between *'s across row → and end last repeat: K 5 (instead of k 9).

Row 7 (right side of work): Knit.

Row 8: Knit.

Row 9: K 5, o, *k 1, o, k 9, o*. Repeat between *'s across row and end: K 1, o, k 5.

Row 10: K 5, o, *k 3, o, k 9, o*. Repeat between *'s across row → and end last repeat: K 5 (instead of k 9, o).

Row 11: Knit a double throw into next 4 sts, *k 1, o, k 5, o, k 1, knit a double throw into next 7 sts*. Repeat between *'s across row → and end last repeat: Knit a double throw into 4 sts (instead of into 7).

Row 12: Sl 4 double throws, slip to left needle and purl tog, *k 9, sl 7, slip to left needle and purl tog*. Repeat between *'s across row → and end last repeat: Slip and purl tog 4 (instead of 7).

PERUVIAN

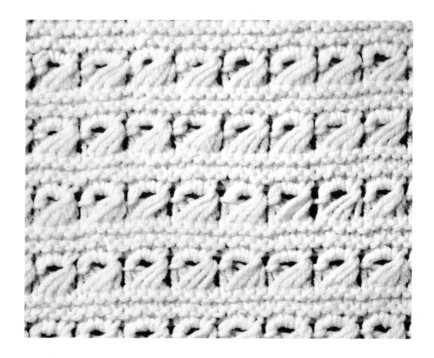

An interesting design that knits up very quickly and has many uses where a loose-knit fabric is needed. Extremely attractive when several blending or contrasting colors are used.

Suggested uses: Stoles, mufflers, ponchos, toga tops, afghans, drapery fabric, place setting mats, lounge wear

Cast on a multiple of 4 stitches plus 2.

Row 1: Knit.

Row 2: Knit.

Row 3: K 1, knit a triple throw into each st across row → and end last st: K 1.

Row 4: K 1, *sl 4 purlwise (keeping yarn to back), inserting point of right needle into first strand to slip and dropping second and third strand from left needle; slip these 4 sts back onto left needle; insert right needle through all 4 sts, as if to knit them all together, then: K 1, p 1, k 1, p 1 into all 4 tog before slipping from left needle*. Repeat between *'s across row and end: K 1.

Row 5: Knit.

Row 6: Knit.

PERUVIAN LACE

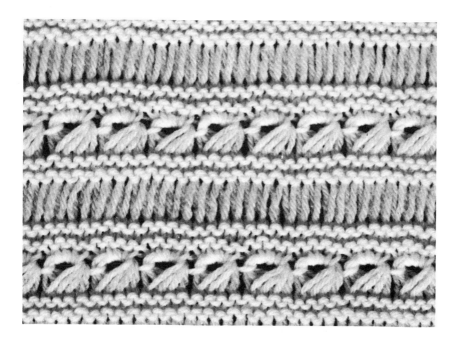

A variation of Peruvian, this unusual design has a startling effect when used as a drapery fabric and knits up very quickly in medium- or heavy-weight yarns.

Suggested uses: Stoles, scarves, tablecloths, lounge wear, drapery fabric, place setting mats

Cast on a multiple of 4 stitches plus 2.

Rows 1 and 2: Knit.

Row 3: K 1, knit a triple throw into each st across row → and end last st: K 1.

Row 4: K 1, *sl 4 purlwise (keeping yarn to back), inserting point of right needle into first strand to slip and dropping second and third strand from left needle; slip these 4 sts back onto left needle; insert right needle through all 4 sts, as if to knit them all together, then: K 1, p 1, k 1, p 1 into all 4 tog, before slipping from left needle*. Repeat between *'s across row and end: K 1.

Rows 5, 6, 7, and 8: Knit.

Row 9: Knit a triple throw into each st across row.

Row 10: Knit, knitting into first strand and dropping second and third strand from left needle.

VALENTINE

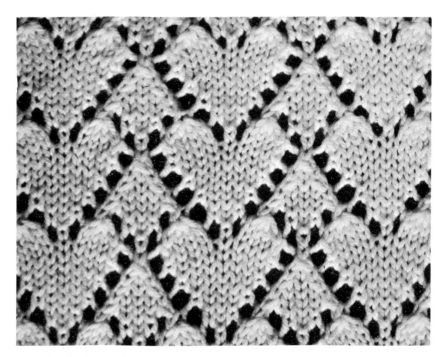

A new design utilizing a heretofore neglected shape, the heart motif. This charming pattern is particularly interesting when knitted in white yarn and lined with a fabric of clear red tone, or vice versa.

Suggested uses: Stoles, scarves, women's and girls' wear, place setting mats, tablecloths, lined upholstery and drapery fabric

Cast on a multiple of 12 stitches plus 1.

Row 1: K 1, *o, k 2 tog, k 3, o, k 1, o, k 3, sl 1, k 1, psso, o, k 1*. Repeat between *'s across row.

Row 2 (and all even-numbered rows): Purl.

Row 3: K 2, *o, k 4 tog, o, k 3*. Repeat between *'s across row → and end last repeat: K 2 (instead of k 3).

Row 5: K 1, *k 1, k 2 tog, o, k 5, o, sl 1, k 1, psso, k 2*. Repeat between *'s across row.

Row 7: K 1, *k 2 tog, o, k 7, o, sl 1, k 1, psso, k 1*. Repeat between *'s across row.

Row 9: K 2 tog, o, k 9, o, *sl 1. k 2 tog, psso, o, k 9, o*. Repeat between *'s across row and end: Sl 1, k 1, psso.

Row 10: Purl.

TULIP TIME

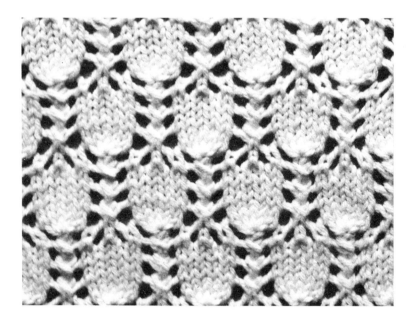

This very charming lacy pattern is an upside-down stitch; it is knitted from top to bottom and becomes a recurring tulip motif when turned. Items with a definite upper and lower edge must be knitted exactly the reverse from most knitted patterns.

Suggested uses: Place setting mats, tablecloths, counterpanes, stoles, shrugs, drapery fabric, upholstery fabric lined with contrasting color

Cast on a multiple of 8 stitches plus 1.

Row 1: K 2 tog, *o, k 5, o, sl 1, k 2 tog, psso*. Repeat between *'s across row → and end last repeat: Sl 1, k 1, psso (instead of k 2 tog, psso).

Row 2 (and all even-numbered rows): Purl.

Rows 3 and 5: Same as Row 1.

Row 7: *K 1, o, k 1, o, k 5 tog, o, k 1, o*. Repeat between *'s across row and end last st: K 1.

Row 9: K 3, *o, sl 1, k 2 tog, psso, o, k 5*. Repeat between *'s across row and end last repeat: K 3.

Rows 11 and 13: Same as Row 9.

Row 15: K 3 tog, *o, (k 1, o) 3 times, k 5 tog*. Repeat between *'s across row → and end last repeat: K 3 tog (instead of k 5 tog).

Row 16: Purl.

KATHERINE

Cast on 12 sts for a single strip of vertical edge motif, or a multiple of 12 sts where a wide expanse is required. (Single strip contains 2 vertical patterns.)

Row 1: *P 2, k 2, p 4, twist 2, p 2*. Work between *'s once, for single strip or edging, or as many times as multiples cast on.
Row 2: Purl.
Row 3: *P 2, twist 2, p 4, (k 1, p 1, k 1) into next st, (k 1, p 1, k 1) into next st, p 2*. Repeat between *'s across row.
Row 4: *P 2, k 6, p 8*. Repeat between *'s across row.
Row 5: *P 2, k 2, p 4, purl a double throw into each of next 6 sts, p 2*. Repeat between *'s across row.
Row 6: *P 2, sl 6 (insert needle purlwise into first strand of each st, slip onto needle without working, and drop second strand, creating a "long stitch" that has been slipped), slip these 6 long sts back onto left needle

and → (k 1, p 1) in all 6 sts tog before slipping from left needle, → p 8*. Repeat between *'s across row.

Row 7: *P 2, twist 2, p 4, k 2, p 2*. Repeat between *'s across row.

Row 8: Purl.

Row 9: Same as Row 1.

Row 10: Purl.

Row 11: Same as Row 7.

Row 12: Purl.

Row 13: *P 2, (k 1, p 1, k 1) into each of next 2 sts (as in Row 3), p 4, twist 2, p 2*. Repeat between *'s across row.

Row 14: *P 8, k 6, p 2*. Repeat between *'s across row.

Row 15: *P 2, purl a double throw into each of next 6 sts, p 4, k 2, p 2*. Repeat between *'s across row.

Row 16: *P 8, sl 6 (long sts, as before) purlwise, return them to left needle, and → (k 1, p 1) into all 6 sts before slipping off left needle → p 2*. Repeat between *'s across row.

Row 17: Same as Row 1.

Row 18: Purl.

Row 19: *P 2, twist 2, p 4, k 2, p 2*. Repeat between *'s across row.

Row 20: Purl.

BELLE

A very attractive, highly embossed bell motif. The directions for working this pattern are so arranged that a single or double pair of motifs can be knitted by casting on only one or two of the required multiples. These panels of Belle are interesting when used as trimming on an otherwise plain garment.

Suggested uses: Afghans, carriage covers, ornamental collars, cuffs and pockets, Bavarian ski sweaters, hats, handbags

Cast on a multiple of 18 stitches.

Row 1: *K 4, (k 1, p 1, k 1, p 1, k 1) into next st before removing from left needle, k 13*. Repeat between *'s across row, bearing in mind that this pattern repeat begins and ends with knit stitches.

Row 2: *K 4, yarn forward, sl 1 purlwise, yarn to back, k 17*.

Row 3: Knit.

Row 4: Same as Row 2.

Row 5: *K 4, knit a double throw into next 5 sts, k 13*.

Row 6: *K 4, yarn forward, sl 1, purlwise, yarn to back, k 8, yarn forward, sl 5 purlwise (slip first strand, drop second strand), yarn to back, k 4*

Row 7: *K 4, sl 5 purlwise (leaving yarn at back), k 13*.

Row 8: *K 4, yarn forward, sl 1, yarn to back, k 8, p 5 tog, k 4*.

Row 9: *K 13, (k 1, p 1, k 1, p 1, k 1) in next st, k 4*.

Row 10: *K 17, yarn forward, sl 1, yarn to back, k 4*.

Row 11: Knit.

Row 12: Same as Row 10.

Row 13: *K 13, knit a double throw into next 5 sts, k 4*.

Row 14: *K 4, yarn forward, sl 5 purlwise, yarn to back, k 8, yarn forward, sl 1 purlwise, yarn to back, k 4*.

Row 15: *K 13, sl 5 purlwise (keeping yarn to back), k 4*.

Row 16: *K 4, p 5 tog, k 8, yarn forward, sl 1 purlwise, yarn to back, k 4*.

BELLFLOWER AND CABLE

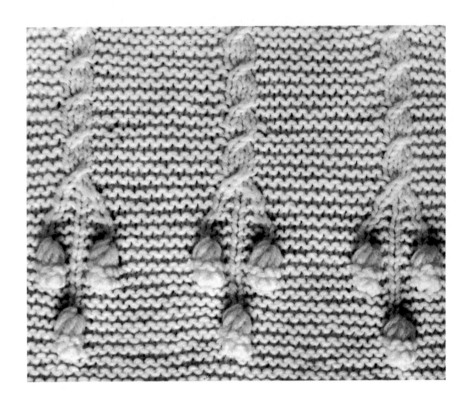

Cast on a multiple of 15 stitches.

Row 1: *K 7, (k 1, p 1, k 1, p 1, k 1, p 1) into next st before dropping it from left needle, k 7*. Repeat between *'s across row, taking careful note that each repeat begins and ends with a k 7.

Rows 2, 3, and 4: Knit.

Row 5: *K 7, knit a double throw into next 6 sts, k 7*. Repeat between *'s across row.

Row 6: *K 7, yarn forward, sl 6 purlwise (insert needle into first strand of each st and slip without working, dropping second strand), yarn to back, k 7*. Repeat between *'s across row.

Row 7: *K 7, sl 6 purlwise, k 7*. Repeat between *'s across row.

Row 8: *K 7, p 6 tog, k 7*. Repeat between *'s across row.

Row 9: Knit.

Row 10: *K 7, p 1, k 7*. Repeat between *'s.

Row 11: Knit.

Row 12: *K 7, p 1, k 7*. Repeat between *'s.

Row 13: *K 4, increase next st to 6 (as in Row 1), k 5, increase next st to 6, k 4*. Repeat between *'s.

Row 14: *K 12, p 1, k 12*. Repeat between *'s.

Row 15: Knit.

Row 16: *K 12, p 1, k 12*. Repeat between *'s.

Row 17: *K 4, knit a double throw into next 6 sts, k 5, knit a double throw into next 6 sts, k 4*. Repeat between *'s.

Row 18: *K 4, yarn forward, sl 6 purlwise (as in Row 6), yarn to back, k 2, p 1, k 2, yarn forward, sl 6 purlwise, yarn to back, k 4*. Repeat between *'s.

Row 19: *K 4, sl 6 purlwise (keeping yarn to back), k 5, sl 6 purlwise (keeping yarn to back), k 4*.

Row 20: *K 4, p 6 tog, k 2, p 1, k 2, p 6 tog, k 4*.

Row 21: Knit.

Row 22: *K 4, p 1, k 2, p 1, k 2, p 1, k 4*.

Row 23: Knit.

Row 24: Same as Row 22.

Row 25: *K 4, twist 2 left, k 3, twist 2 right, k 4*.

Row 26: *K 5, p 1, k 1, p 1, k 1, p 1, k 5*.

Row 27: Knit.

Row 28: Same as Row 26.

Row 29: *K 5, twist 2 left, k 1, twist 2 right, k 5*.

Row 30: *K 6, p 3, k 6*.

→ End of Bellflower; work Baby Cable Twist Pattern (below) for desired length.

Row 1: *K 6, twist 3, k 6*. Repeat between *'s across row.

Row 2: *K 6, p 3, k 6*. Repeat.

Row 3: Knit.

Row 4: *K 6, p 3, k 6*.

Row 5: Knit.

Row 6: *K 6, p 3, k 6*.

SNOWDROP

A useful and attractive vertical motif which can be used as a single strip or a broad expanse of fabric; it is highly embossed and turns out well in fine yarns as well as in the heavier types.

Suggested uses: Women's cardigans, afghan strips, wool or cotton coverlets, decorator pillows, hats, handbags, decorative panels

Cast on a multiple of 15 stitches.

Row 1: *P 4, (k 1, p 1, k 1, p 1) in next st (before slipping from left needle), k 2, sl 1 purlwise, k 3, p 4*. Repeat between *'s across row, noting that each repeat begins and ends with a p 4 on all odd-numbered rows.

Row 2: *P 10, k 4, p 4*. Repeat between *'s across row.

Row 3: *P 4, purl a double throw into next 4 sts, k 2, sl 1 purlwise, k 3, p 4*.

Row 4: *P 10, sl 4 purlwise (slip first strand, drop second), p 4*.

Row 5: *P 4, slip next 4 sts onto cable needle and to front of work, k 2, slip 4 sts on cable needle back onto left needle and knit these 4 sts tog through back of loops, sl 1 purlwise, k 3, p 4*.

Row 6: Purl.

Row 7: *P 4, k 3, sl 1 purlwise, k 2, (k 1, p 1, k 1, p 1) into next st, p 4*.

Row 8: *P 4, k 4, p 10*.

Row 9: *P 4, k 3, sl 1 purlwise, k 2, purl a double throw into next 4 sts, p 4*.

Row 10: *P 4, sl 4 purlwise, p 10*.

Row 11: *P 4, k 3, sl 1 purlwise, slip next 2 sts onto cable needle and drop to back of work, knit next 4 sts tog through front of loops, knit the 2 sts on cable needle, p 4*.

Row 12: Purl.

NEEDLEWORK BAG in Snowdrop Pattern

Materials required: 2 4-oz skeins 4-ply knitting worsted or any other suitable yarn yielding the same stitch gauge, 1 pair ✕7 knitting needles, 1 pair ✕8 knitting needles, 1 round plastic or cardboard bucket-shaped container measuring approximately 8½″ across the top and 8½″ high (size can vary slightly); these cardboard or plastic containers can be obtained in paint or hardware stores.

Stitch gauge on ✕8 needles: 4½ stitches equal 1″.

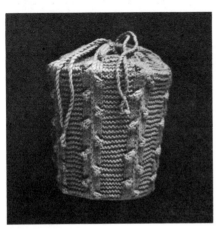

Using ✕7 needles, cast on 120 sts and work in k 1, p 1 ribbing for 2½″, then work in Snowdrop Pattern for 2½″. Change to ✕8 needles and continue in pattern until work measures 14½″ from beginning, including the ribbing. With right side of fabric facing, knit a double throw into each stitch across row. Draw a strand of yarn through these stitches (instead of binding them off), inserting yarn needle into first strand and dropping second strand of double throw. Break working yarn several inches from fabric and fasten securely. Sew side edges together from top to bottom and fasten securely; then, before breaking the sewing yarn, sew a running stitch around cast-on stitches (below ribbing), pull up to 1½″ diameter, and fasten. Wet thoroughly in lukewarm water, squeeze excess moisture out, and roll in a terry-cloth towel and leave for a few minutes, then place needlework bag over cardboard or plastic bucket to dry. Make 2 8-strand cords each 1 yd long. Starting at seam side, run cord through double throw stitches, removing strand, and tie the 2 ends of cord together in a single knot. Starting at opposite side of seam, run the second cord through stitches and tie as for first cord. Pull each cord in opposite directions to draw up and close top.

MADEIRA

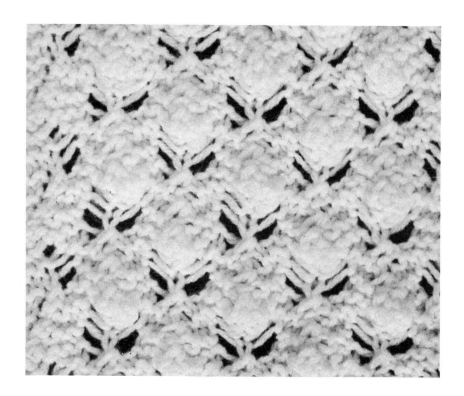

Cast on a multiple of 12 stitches plus 5.

Rows 1, 2, 3, 4, 5, and 6: K 2, *k 1, o, k 4, p 3 tog, k 4, o*. Repeat between *'s across row and end: K 3.

Rows 7, 8, 9, 10, 11, and 12: K 2, p 2 tog, *k 4, o, k 1, o, k 4, p 3 tog*. Repeat between *'s across row → and end last repeat: P 2 tog (instead of p 3 tog), k 2.

DIAMOND QUILT

One of the most useful and attractive of the winter-weight fabrics, it is both masculine and feminine as well as being domestically neutral.

Suggested uses: Cardigans, pullovers, jackets, walking coats, hot mats, place setting mats, decorator pillows, drapery and upholstery fabric, ornamental collars, cuffs, pockets, panels, edgings, hats, handbags, afghan squares, scatter rugs, bath mats

Cast on a multiple of 6 stitches plus 2. All sl sts are done purlwise.

Row 1: P 1, *o, p 5, o, p 1*. Repeat between *'s across row and end: P 1.

Row 2: K 1, *st 1, drop o from left needle, k 4, sl 1, drop o*. Repeat between *'s across row and end: K 1.

Row 3: P 1, *sl 1, p 4, sl 1*. Repeat between *'s across row and end: P 1.

Row 4: K 1, *sl 1, k 4, sl 1*. Repeat between *'s across row and end: K 1.

Row 5: Same as Row 3.

Row 6: K 1, *drop next st, k 2, pick up dropped st and knit, sl 2, drop next st, slip the 2 sl sts back onto left needle, knit the dropped st, k 2*. Repeat between *'s across row and end: K 1. → Care should be taken not to twist the long sts when picking up to knit; each st should lie flat at base.

Row 7: P 1, *p 2, o, p 1, o, p 3*. Repeat between *'s across row and end: P 1.

Row 8: K 1, *k 2, sl 1, drop o, sl 1, drop o, k 2*. Repeat between *'s across row and end: K 1.

Row 9: P 1, *p 2, sl 2, p 2*. Repeat between *'s across row and end: P 1.

Row 10: K 1, *k 2, sl 2, k 2*. Repeat between *'s across row and end: K 1.

Row 11: Same as Row 9.

Row 12: K 1, *sl 2, drop next st, slip the 2 sl sts back onto left needle, knit the dropped st, k 2, drop next st, k 2, knit the dropped st*. Repeat between *'s across row and end: K 1.

DOVES ON THE WING

In this unusual design, one can see doves flying in wing-tip formation across each pattern unit of this extremely attractive winter-weight fabric. It is very useful as a warm, heavy material and at the same time ornamental enough for high-fashion apparel.

Suggested uses: Winter walking coats and other women's wear, hot mats, place setting mats, alternating afghan strips, hats, handbags, tote bags, ornamental pockets, collars, cuffs, panels, edgings

Cast on a multiple of 6 stitches plus 2.

Row 1 (right side): Purl.

Row 2: P 1, purl a double throw into next st, *p 4, purl a double throw into next 2 sts*. Repeat between *'s across row → and end last repeat: Purl a double throw into next st, p 1.

Row 3: K 1, sl 1 (leaving yarn at back, slip st purlwise into first strand, slipping second strand from left needle without working), *k 4,

sl 2 purlwise*. Repeat between *'s across row → and end last repeat:
Sl 1, k 1 (instead of sl 2).

Row 4: P 1, sl 1 purlwise (leaving yarn at back), *p 4, sl 2 purlwise
(leaving yarn at back)*. Repeat between *'s across row → and end last
repeat: Sl 1, p 1 (instead of sl 2).

Row 5: K 1, sl 1, *k 4, sl 2 purlwise (leaving yarn at back)*. Repeat
between *'s across row → and end last repeat: Sl 1 purlwise, k 1
(instead of sl 2).

Row 6: Same as Row 4.

Row 7: K 1, *drop long st from needle, k 2, pick up long st on left
needle and knit, sl 2, drop next long st, return the 2 slipped sts to left
needle, pick up long st and knit, k 2*. Repeat between *'s across row
and end: K 1.

Row 8: Knit across row.

PUFFIN

A very old favorite, dating back to the late Victorian period; it is simple to do and most beginners will have no trouble working this very popular pattern.

Suggested uses: Hats, handbags, alternating afghan squares, hot mats, place setting mats, coverlets, slipper tops, baby items, upholstery and drapery fabric, decorator pillows

Cast on a multiple of 8 stitches plus 3.

Row 1: K 5, *yarn forward, sl 5 purlwise, k 3*. Repeat between *'s across row → and end last repeat K 1 (instead of k 3).

Row 2 (and all even-numbered rows): Purl.

Row 3: Same as Row 1.

Row 5: Same as Row 1.

Row 7: K 7, *insert right needle up through slip strands, knit next st and draw loop under strands, k 7*. Repeat between *'s across row → and end last repeat: K 3 (instead of k 7).

Row 9: K 1, *yarn forward, sl 5 purlwise, k 3*. Repeat between *'s across row and end: K 2.

Row 11: Same as Row 9.

Row 13: Same as Row 9.

Row 15: K 3, *right needle through slip strands (as in Row 7), k 1, draw loop through strands, k 7*. Repeat between *'s across row.

Row 16: Purl.

III
INTRICATE AND ELEGANT

CANDLELIGHT

A cool, crisp, and altogether lovely old pattern that dates back to the early Victorian period and is still a delight to knitters.

Suggested uses: Women's spring- and summer-weight wear, place setting mats, tablecloths, stoles, scarves, drapery fabric, lined upholstery fabric, alternating afghan squares

Cast on a multiple of 10 stitches plus 1.

Row 1: K 1, *o, sl 1, k 1, psso, k 5, k 2 tog, o, k 1*. Repeat between *'s across row.

Row 2 (and all even-numbered rows): Purl.

Row 3: K 1, *o, k 1, sl 1, k 1, psso, k 3, k 2 tog, k 1, o, k 1*. Repeat between *'s across row.

Row 5: K 1, *o, k 2, sl 1, k 1, psso, k 1, k 2 tog, k 2, o, k 1*. Repeat between *'s across row.

Row 7: K 1, *o, k 3, sl 1, k 2 tog, psso, k 3, o, k 1*. Repeat between *'s across row.

Row 9: K 1, *k 2, k 2 tog, o, k 1, o, sl 1, k 1, psso, k 3*. Repeat between *'s across row.

Row 11: K 1, *k 1, k 2 tog, k 1, o, k 1, o, k 1, sl 1, k 1, psso, k 2*. Repeat between *'s across row.

Row 13: K 1, *k 2 tog, k 2, o, k 1, o, k 2, sl 1, k 1, psso, k 1*. Repeat between *'s across row.

Row 15: Sl 1, k 1, psso, *k 3, o, k 1, o, k 3, sl 1, k 2 tog, psso*. Repeat between *'s across row and end: Sl 1, k 1, psso.

Row 16: Purl.

BLOUSE in Candlelight Pattern

Materials required: 3 4-oz skeins 4-ply knitting worsted, 1 pair ✕9 knitting needles, 1 ✕00 crochet hook

Stitch gauge: 9 sts equal 2″.

Make 2 (front and back are identical):

> For size 34–36 cast on 81 sts.
> For size 38–40 cast on 91 sts.

Work in Candlelight Pattern until fabric measures 14″ from beginning.

SHAPE SLEEVES: Cast on 10 sts at beginning of next 8 rows (counting both front and reverse sides as rows) for sleeves, taking care to follow pattern. This will total 40 added sts on EACH side for sleeves. When sleeve measures 8½″ at widest part (underarm) bind off all sts loosely.

ASSEMBLING AND FINISHING: Sew sleeve and shoulder seams, leaving a 10″ opening in the middle for neckline. Sew underarm and side seams. Using ✕00 crochet hook, work 3 rows of single crochet around lower edge, neckline, and lower edge of sleeves. Crochet a simple chain 11″ long, tie into a bow, and fasten at center of neckline. Block to exact measurements.

LACY CABLE

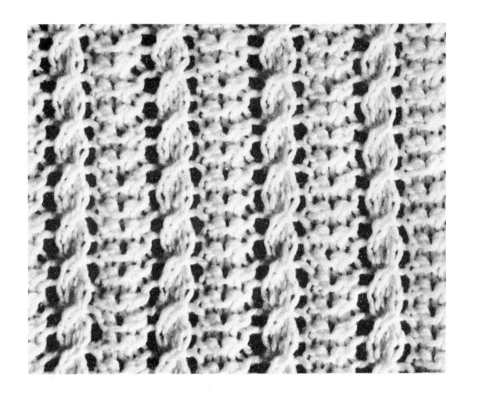

Cast on a multiple of 7 stitches; use a needle size 2 or 3 times larger than would ordinarily be used.

Row 1: *P 2 tog, lift-increase 1 purlwise, k 3, lift-increase 1 purlwise, p 2 tog*. Repeat across row.
Row 2: Purl.
Row 3: *P 2 tog, lift-increase 1 purlwise, twist 3, lift-increase 1 purl-wise, p 2 tog*. Repeat across row.
Row 4: Purl.

FALLING LEAF

Cast on a multiple of 8 stitches plus 1.

Row 1: K 3, *o, sl 1, k 2 tog, psso, o, k 5*. Repeat between *'s across row → and end last repeat: K 3 (instead of k 5).

Row 2 (and all even-numbered rows): Purl.

Row 3: K 2 tog, k 1, *o, k 3, o, k 1, sl 1, k 2 tog, psso, k 1*. Repeat between *'s across row and end: O, k 3, o, k 1, k 2 tog.

Row 5: K 2 tog, *o, k 5, o, sl 1, k 2 tog, psso*. Repeat between *'s across row and end: O, k 5, o, k 2 tog.

Row 7: K 2, *o, k 1, sl 1, k 2 tog, psso, k 1, o, k 3*. Repeat between *'s across row → and end last repeat: K 2 (instead of k 3).

Row 8: Purl.

PALM LEAF

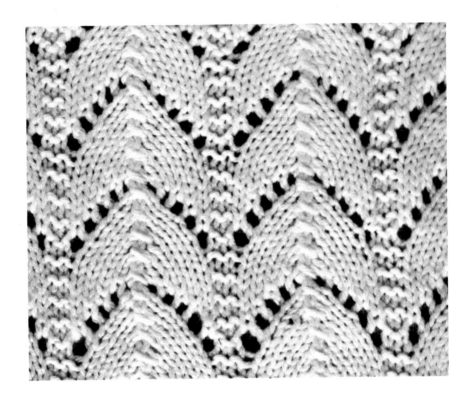

This particular adaptation has been streamlined from a very old version and probably dates back to the seventeenth century. Widely used during the Victorian era, this simplified version remains substantially the same in design, but with far less knitting acrobatics to achieve it.

Suggested uses: Women's wear, afghans, coverlets, lounge wear, tablecloths, place setting mats, ornamental inserts

Cast on a multiple of 13 stitches plus 5.

Row 1: P 2, sl 1, k 1, psso, k 4, o, *p 2, o, k 4, sl 1, k 2 tog, psso, k 4, o*. Repeat between *'s across row and end: P 2, o, k 4, k 2 tog, p 2.

Row 2 (and all even-numbered rows): Purl.

Row 3: P 2, sl 1, k 1, psso, k 3, o, k 1, *p 2, k 1, o, k 3, sl 1, k 2 tog, psso, k 3, o, k 1*. Repeat between *'s across row and end: P 2, k 1, o, k 3, k 2 tog, p 2.

Row 5: P 2, sl 1, k 1, psso, k 2, o, k 2, *p 2, k 2, o, k 2, sl 1, k 2 tog, psso, k 2, o, k 2*. Repeat between *'s across row and end: P 2, k 2, o, k 2, k 2 tog, p 2.

Row 7: P 2, sl 1, k 1, psso, k 1, o, k 3, *p 2, k 3, o, k 1, sl 1, k 2 tog, psso, k 1, o, k 3*. Repeat between *'s across row and end: P 2, k 3, o, k 1, k 2 tog, p 2.

Row 9: P 2, sl 1, k 1, psso, o, k 4, *p 2, k 4, o, sl 1, k 2 tog, psso, o, k 4*. Repeat between *'s across row and end: P 2, k 4, o, k 2 tog, p 2.

Row 10: Purl.

PINE TREE

Cast on a multiple of 12 stitches plus 1.

Row 1: *K 1, o, k 1, sl 1, k 1, psso, k 5, k 2 tog, k 1, o*. Repeat between *'s across row and end: K 1.
Rows 2, 4, and 6: Purl.
Row 3: *K 2, o, k 1, sl 1, k 1, psso, k 3, k 2 tog, k 1, o, k 1*. Repeat between *'s across row and end: K 1.
Row 5: *K 3, o, k 1, sl 1, k 1, psso, k 1, k 2 tog, k 1, o, k 2*. Repeat between *'s across row and end: K 1.
Row 7: *K 4, o, k 1, sl 1, k 2 tog, psso, k 1, o, k 3*. Repeat between *'s across row and end: K 1.
Row 8: Purl.

FERN

This delicate lacy pattern has been widely used for centuries, particularly during the Victorian era, for bedspreads, antimacassars, and other items of the "white knitting" period.

Suggested uses: Tablecloths, place setting mats, scarves, stoles, alternating afghan strips, dresses, and blouses

Cast on a multiple of 18 stitches plus 2.

Row 1: P 2, *k 2 tog, k 2, o, k 5, o, k 2, sl 1, k 1, psso, k 3, p 2*. Repeat between *'s across row.

Row 2 (and all even-numbered rows). Purl.

Row 3: P 2, *k 5, k 2 tog, k 2, o, k 1, o, k 2, sl 1, k 1, psso, k 2, p 2*. Repeat between *'s across row.

Row 5: P 2, *k 4, k 2 tog, k 2, o, k 3, o, k 2, sl 1, k 1, psso, k 1, p 2*. Repeat between *'s across row.

Row 7: P 2, *k 3, k 2 tog, k 2, o, k 5, o, k 2 sl 1 k 1, psso, p 2*. Repeat between *'s across row.

Row 9: P 2, *k 2, k 2 tog, k 2, o, k 1, o, k 2, sl 1, k 1, psso, k 5, p 2*. Repeat between *'s across row.

Row 11: P 2, *k 1, k 2 tog, k 2, o, k 3, o, k 2, sl 1, k 1, psso, k 4, p 2*. Repeat between *'s across row.

Row 12: Purl.

PRIMROSE LACE

Although a new design in its present form, this beautiful pattern is a type of knitted lace that dates back to the fifteenth century and was widely used by silk knitters' guilds for hosiery and lingerie.

Suggested uses: Stoles, scarves, dresses and blouses, place setting mats, tablecloths, and very decorative when used as a drapery and upholstery fabric lined with a contrasting color

Cast on a multiple of 12 stitches plus 1.

Row 1: *K 5, o, sl 1, k 2 tog, psso, o, k 4*. Repeat between *'s across row and end: K 1.

Row 2 (and all even-numbered rows): Purl.

Row 3: K 2 tog, *k 3, o, k 3, o, k 3, sl 1, k 2 tog, psso*. Repeat between *'s across row → and end last repeat: Sl 1, k 1, psso (instead of sl 1, k 2 tog, psso).

Row 5: K 2 tog, *k 2, o, k 5, o, k 2, sl 1, k 2 tog, psso*. Repeat between *'s across row and end → last repeat: Sl 1, k 1, psso (instead of sl 1, k 2 tog, psso).

Row 7: K 2 tog, *k 1, o, k 7, o, k 1, sl 1, k 2 tog, psso*. Repeat between *'s across row → and end last repeat: Sl 1, k 1, psso (instead of sl 1, k 2 tog, psso).

Row 9: K 2 tog, *o, k 3, o, sl 1, k 2 tog, psso*. Repeat between *'s across row → and end last repeat: Sl 1, k 1, psso (instead of sl 1, k 2 tog, psso).

Row 11: Sl 1, k 1, psso, *o, k 3 tog, o, (k 1, o) 3 times, k 3 tog, o, sl 2 tog, k 1, pass the 2 sl sts (tog) over the knit st*. Repeat between *'s across row → and end last repeat: K 2 tog (instead of passing 2 sl sts over k st).

Row 13: *K 1, k 2 tog, o, k 7, o, sl 1, k 1, psso*. Repeat between *'s across row and end: K 1.

Row 15: *K 3, o, sl 1, k 2 tog, psso, o, k 1, o, sl 1, k 2 tog, psso, o, k 2*. Repeat between *'s across row and end: K 1.

Row 17: *K 3, k 2 tog, o, k 3, o, sl 1, k 1, psso, k 2*. Repeat between *'s across row and end: K 1.

Row 18: Purl.

ROSE LEAF LACE

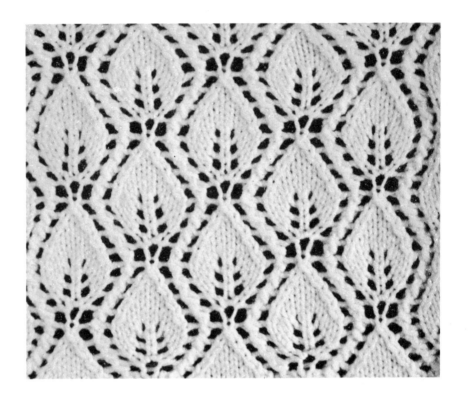

A new design from an old Victorian motif. It adapts itself well to any weight wool, synthetic, or cotton yarn and is always a conversation piece when used in decorative household items.

Suggested uses: Scarves, stoles, place setting mats, tablecloths, drapery fabric, bedspreads, decorative centerpieces, upholstery fabric lined with contrasting color

Cast on a multiple of 16 sts plus 1.

Row 1: (P 1, k 1) in first st, *o, sl 1, k 2 tog, psso, o, sl 1, k 1, psso, k 5, k 2 tog, o, sl 1, k 2 tog, psso, o, (k 1, p 1, k 1) in next st*. Repeat between *'s across row → and end last repeat: (K 1, p 1) in last st → (instead of k 1, p 1, k 1).

Row 2 (and all even-numbered rows): Purl across row, purling all overs (o) and 3-in-1 sts as separate sts.

Row 3: K 1, o, k 1, o, *sl 1, k 2 tog, psso, o, sl 1, k 1, psso, k 3, k 2 tog o, sl 1, k 2 tog, psso, o, (k 1, o) 3 times*. Repeat between *'s across row → and end last repeat: K 1, o, k 1.

Row 5: K 1, o, k 2, *o, sl 1, k 2 tog, psso, o, sl l, k 1, psso, k 1, k 2 tog, o, sl 1, k 2 tog, psso, o, k 2, o, k 1, o, k 2*. Repeat between *'s across row → and end last repeat: K 1 (instead of k 1, o, k 2).

Row 7: K 1, o, k 3, *o, sl 1, k 2 tog, psso, o, sl 1, k 2 tog, psso, o, sl 1, k 2 tog, psso, o, k 3, o, k 1, o, k 3*. Repeat between *'s across row → and end last repeat: O, k 1 (instead of o, k 1, o, k 3).

Row 9: K 3, *k 2 tog, o, sl 1, k 2 tog, psso, o, (k 1, p 1, k 1) in next st, o, sl 1, k 2 tog, psso, o, sl 1, k 1, psso, k 5*. Repeat between *'s across row → and end last repeat: K 3 (instead of k 5).

Row 11: K 2, *k 2 tog, o, sl 1, k 2 tog, psso, o, (k 1, o) 3 times, sl 1, k 2 tog, psso, o, sl 1, k 1, psso, k 3*. Repeat between *'s across row → and end last repeat: K 2 (instead of k 3).

Row 13: *K 1, k 2 tog, o, sl 1, k 2 tog, psso, o, k 2, o, k 1, o, k 2, o, sl 1, k 2 tog, psso, o, sl 1, k 1, psso*. Repeat between *'s across row and end: K 1.

Row 15: K 2 tog, *o, sl 1, k 2 tog, psso, o, k 3, o, k 1, o, k 3, o, sl 1, k 2 tog, psso, o, sl 1, k 2 tog, psso*. Repeat between *'s across row → and end last repeat: O, sl 1, k 1, psso (instead of o, sl 1, k 2 tog, psso).

Row 16: Purl.

LUNCHEON CLOTH AND TABLECLOTHS
in Rose Leaf Lace Pattern

1. **Luncheon cloth, approximate size:** 30″ square

   Materials required: 1 pair ✳6 knitting needles, ✳1 crochet hook, 8 balls (250 yds each) mercerized bedspread cotton (used double strand throughout). Cast on 161 sts

2. **Tablecloth, approximate size:** 32″×40″

   Materials required: 1 pair ✳6 knitting needles, ✳1 crochet hook, 12 balls (250 yds each) mercerized bedspread cotton (used double strand throughout). Cast on 177 sts.

3. **Tablecloth, approximate size:** 40″×60″

   Materials required: 1 pair ✳6 knitting needles, ✳1 crochet hook, 22 balls (250 yds each) mercerized bedspread cotton (used double strand throughout). Cast on 209 sts.

Using 2 strands of cotton together, cast on the required number of sts (according to size of cloth desired, above) and work in Rose Leaf Lace Pattern until work measures:

$$29\frac{1}{2}″ \text{ for size } ✳1$$
$$39\frac{1}{2}″ \text{ for size } ✳2$$
$$59\frac{1}{2}″ \text{ for size } ✳3$$

Bind off all sts loosely.

Using ✳1 crochet hook and double-strand cotton, work 3 rows of single crochet around entire edge of cloth, working 3 single crochet sts in each corner on every row. Launder and press on reverse side, using spray starch according to directions on container, if desired.

ALPINE

Cast on a multiple of 10 sts plus 1.

Row 1: K 4, *k 2 tog, o, k 8*. Repeat between *'s across row → and end last repeat: K 5 (instead of k 8).

Row 2 (and all even-numbered rows): Purl.

Row 3: K 3, *k 2 tog, o, k 1, o, sl 1, k 1, psso, k 5*. Repeat between *'s across row → and end last repeat: K 3 (instead of k 5).

Row 5: K 2, *k 2 tog, o, k 3, o, sl 1, k 1, psso, k 3*. Repeat between *'s across row → and end last repeat: K 2 (instead of k 3).

Row 7: K 1, *k 2 tog, o, k 1, o, sl 1, k 2 tog, psso, o, k 1, o, sl 1, k 1, psso, k 1*. Repeat between *'s across row.

Row 9: K 2 tog, o, k 7, *o, sl 1, k 2 tog, psso, o, k 7*. Repeat between *'s across row and end: O, sl 1, k 1, psso.

Row 10: Purl.

PLACE SETTING MAT in Alpine Pattern

Materials required: 1 pair ✳8 knitting needles, 1 ✳0 crochet hook, 6 large balls (400 yds each) mercerized bedspread cotton for each set of 6 mats

Approximate size of mat:
12"✕18"

Using 3 strands of cotton together as 1, cast on 81 sts and work in Alpine Pattern until fabric measures 12" from beginning. Bind off all sts loosely.

Using ✳0 crochet hook, work 3 rows of single crochet around edges of mat, working 3 single crochet sts in each of the 4 corners of mat every row.

Launder and press before using. Use spray starch, if desired, according to directions on container.

DIAMOND FILIGREE

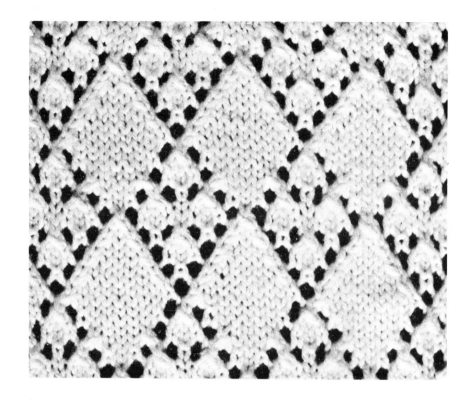

A new and vastly simplified version of a lace design dating back to the fifteenth century, this attractive pattern was combined with other lacy stitches and worked in the finest cotton and linen threads.

Suggested uses: Summer dresses, cardigans, blouses, stoles, shrugs, lounge wear, tablecloths, place setting mats, decorative centerpieces, counterpanes, drapery fabric, upholstery fabric lined with a contrasting color

Cast on a multiple of 10 stitches plus 1.

Row 1: K 4, *k 2 tog, o, k 8*. Repeat between *'s across row → and end last repeat: K 5 (instead of k 8).

Row 2 (and all even-numbered rows): Purl.

Row 3: K 3, *k 2 tog, o, k 1, o, sl 1, k 1, psso, k 5*. Repeat between *'s across row → and end last repeat: K 3 (instead of k 5).

Row 5: K 2, *k 2 tog, o, k 3, o, sl 1, k 1, psso, k 3*. Repeat between *'s across row → and end last repeat: K 2 (instead of k 3).

Row 7:   K 1, *k 2 tog, o, k 1, o, sl 1, k 2 tog, psso, o, k 1, o, sl 1, k 1, psso, k 1*. Repeat between *'s across row.

Row 9:   K 2 tog, *o, k 7, o, sl 1, k 2 tog, psso*. Repeat between *'s across row → and end last repeat: Sl 1, k 1, psso (instead of sl 1, k 2 tog, psso).

Row 11:   K 2, *o, sl 1, k 2 tog, psso, o, k 1, o, sl 1, k 2 tog, psso, o, k 3*. Repeat between *'s across row → and end last repeat: K 2 (instead of k 3).

Row 13:   K 2, *k 2 tog, o, k 3, o, sl 1, k 1, psso, k 3*. Repeat between *'s across row → and end last repeat: K 2 (instead of k 3).

Row 15:   K 4, *o, sl 1, k 2 tog, psso, o, k 7*. Repeat between *'s across row → and end last repeat: K 4 (instead of k 7).

Row 16:   Purl.

TOGA TOP in Diamond Filigree or Alpine Pattern

This attractive Toga Top can be made without any shaping whatsoever by simply casting on 81 stitches, using needle sizes as specified, and working in pattern until the fabric is approximately as long as it is wide. The illustration is in Diamond Filigree Pattern, but this easily made item can also be knitted in Alpine, using the same directions.

If another pattern is desired, the number of stitches to be cast on can be determined in the following way: Using the same yarn and knitting needles that will be used to make the garment, cast on enough multiples of the desired pattern stitch so that swatch will be at least 5″ wide. Work in pattern until swatch measures 4½″ from the beginning. Bind off all stitches loosely. Dip swatch in lukewarm water until thoroughly wet. Squeeze gently until excess moisture is removed, and roll in terry-cloth towel. Allow to remain in towel for a few minutes, then remove and smooth out on a flat surface. Allow swatch to dry thoroughly in this position, then press lightly on the reverse side with iron set at wool temperature. Using a metal tape measure or a ruler, measure the exact number of stitches to 1″ of fabric. Measure bust loosely. Divide the number of inches in bust measurement in half. Now multiply this number (half of bust measurement inches) times the number of stitches to 1″ of knitted fabric. The result will be the approximate number of stitches to be cast on. Stitches can be added or subtracted up to 3 or 4 in order to adjust to the number of stitches in pattern multiple. Cast on this adjusted number of stitches and follow the general directions given for Toga Top.

Materials required: 3 4-oz skeins 4-ply knitting worsted, 1 pair of knitting needles, sizes as specified below, 1 ✗00 crochet hook

1 pair ✗8 needles for size 34–36
1 pair ✗9 needles for size 38–40

Stitch gauge: ✕8 needles, 9 sts equal 2″.

✕9 needles, 8½ sts equal 2″.

MAKE 2: Cast on 81 sts and work in Diamond Filigree or Alpine Pattern until fabric is slightly longer than it is wide (or desired length from shoulder seam to lower edge). Complete pattern to last numbered row and bind off all sts loosely.

ASSEMBLING AND FINISHING: Work 3 rows of single crochet around all 4 sides of each piece, working 3 single crochet sts in each corner every row. Sew shoulder seams, leaving a 10″ opening for neckline. Sew side seams, leaving a 6½″ mandarin slit at lower edges (see photo) and leaving a

7¼″ arm opening for size 34–36

8″ arm opening for size 38–40

Using a double strand of knitting worsted, crochet a simple chain 38″ long (or desired length). Tie a knot in each end of this chain and run in and out of pattern stitch at front, as illustrated, and leaving chain at outside of back. Block to exact measurements.

PYRAMID

A moderately lacy design that is very decorative and useful where a recurring motif in horizontal rows is needed.

Suggested uses: Borders and edgings, women's wear, stoles, scarves, coverlets, drapery fabric, place setting mats

Cast on a multiple of 8 stitches plus 1.

Rows 1 and 2: Knit.

Row 3: K 1, *o, sl 1, k 1, psso, k 3, k 2 tog, o, k 1*. Repeat between *'s across row.

Row 4: Purl.

Row 5: K 2, *o, sl 1, k 1, psso, k 1, k 2 tog, o, k 3*. Repeat between *'s across row → and end last repeat: K 2 (instead of k 3).

Row 6: Purl.

Row 7: K 3, *o, sl 1, k 2 tog, psso, o, k 5*. Repeat between *'s across row → and end last repeat: K 3 (instead of k 5).

Row 8: Knit.

PYRAMID LACE

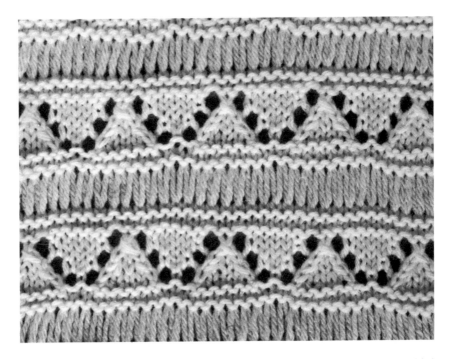

A variation of Pyramid, this interesting design adapts well to high-fashion apparel as well as interior décor items.

Suggested uses: Ponchos, toga tops, redingotes, stoles, robes, drapery fabric, place setting mats, coverlets

Cast on a multiple of 8 stitches plus 1.

Rows 1 and 2: Knit.
Row 3: K 1, *o, sl 1, k 1, psso, k 3, k 2 tog, o, k 1*. Repeat between *'s across row.
Row 4: Purl.
Row 5: K 2, *o, sl 1, k 1, psso, k 1, k 2 tog, o, k 3*. Repeat between *'s across row → and end last repeat: K 2 (instead of k 3).
Row 6: Purl.
Row 7: K 3, *o, sl 1, k 2 tog, psso, o, k 5*. Repeat between *'s across row → and end last repeat: K 3 (instead of k 5).
Rows 8, 9, and 10: Knit.
Row 11: K 1, knit a triple throw into each st across row.
Row 12: Knit, knitting the first strand of each triple throw and dropping second and third strand.

FLOWER GARDEN

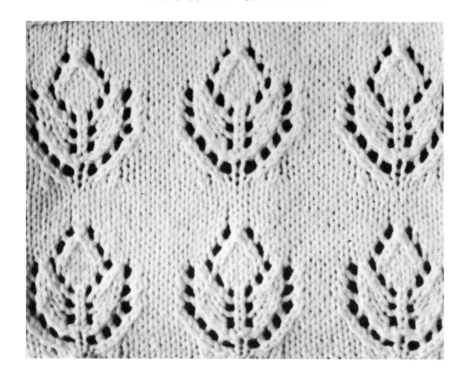

An attractive design with a multitude of uses; very charming when lined with a contrasting color to set off the filet flowers.

Suggested uses: Lined upholstery fabric, drapery fabric, women's wear, ornamental collars, cuffs, pockets

Cast on a multiple of 16 stitches plus 1.

Row 1: Knit.

Row 2 (and all even-numbered rows): Purl.

Row 3: K 1, *k 3, (k 2 tog) twice, o, (k 1, p 1, k 1) in next st, o, sl 1, k 1, psso, sl 1, k 1, psso, k 4*. Repeat between *'s across row.

Row 5: K 1, *k 3, k 2 tog, o, k 2 tog, o, k 1, o, sl 1, k 1, psso, o, sl 1, k 1, psso, k 4*. Repeat between *'s across row.

Row 7: K 1, *k 2, k 2 tog, o, k 2 tog, k 1, o, k 1, o, k 1, sl 1, k 1, psso, o, sl 1, k 1, psso, k 3*. Repeat between *'s across row.

Row 9: K 1, *k 1, k 2 tog, o, k 2 tog, k 2, o, k 1, o, k 2, sl 1, k 1, psso, o, sl 1, k 1, psso, k 2*. Repeat between *'s across row.

Row 11: K 1, *k 1, k 2 tog, o, k 1, k 2 tog, o, k 3, o, sl 1, k 1, psso, k 1, o, sl 1, k 1, psso, k 2*. Repeat between *'s across row.

Row 13: K 1, *k 1, k 2 tog, o, k 2 tog, o, k 5, o, sl 1, k 1, psso, o, sl 1, k 1, psso, k 2*. Repeat between *'s across row.

Row 15: K 1, *k 5, o, sl 1, k 1, psso, k 1, k 2 tog, o, k 6*. Repeat between *'s across row.

Row 17: K 1, *k 6, o, sl 1, k 2 tog, psso, o, k 7*. Repeat between *'s across row.

Row 19: Knit.

Row 21: Knit.

Row 22: Purl.

BOUQUET

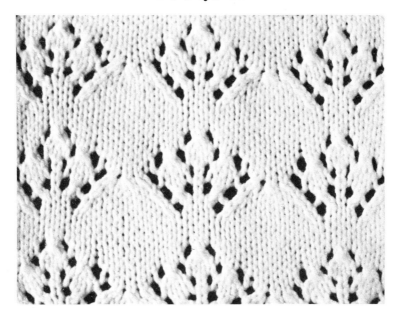

A see-through pattern that is at its best when lined with a fabric of contrasting color.

Suggested uses: Upholstery and drapery fabric, women's and girl's wear, carriage covers, ornamental collars, cuffs, pockets

Cast on a multiple of 14 stitches plus 1.

Row 1: Knit.

Row 2 (and all even-numbered rows): Purl.

Row 3: K 1, *k 3, k 2 tog, o, k 3, o, sl 1, k 1, psso, k 4*. Repeat between *'s across row.

Row 5: K 1, *k 2, k 2 tog, o, k 2 tog, o, k 1, o, sl 1, k 1, psso, o, sl 1, k 1, psso, k 3*. Repeat between *'s across row.

Row 7: K 2 tog, *k 2 tog, o, k 3, o, k 1, o, k 3, o, sl 1, k 1, psso, sl 2, k 1, psso*. Repeat between *'s across row → and end last repeat: Sl 1, k 1, psso.

Row 9: K 1, *k 2, o, k 3 tog, o, k 3, o, sl 1, sl 1, k 1, psso, o, k 3*. Repeat between *'s across row.

Row 11: K 1, *k 5, o, sl 2 tog, k 1, psso, o, k 6*. Repeat between *'s across row.

Row 12: Purl.

Row 13: Knit.

Row 14: Purl.

CABLE AND LEAF

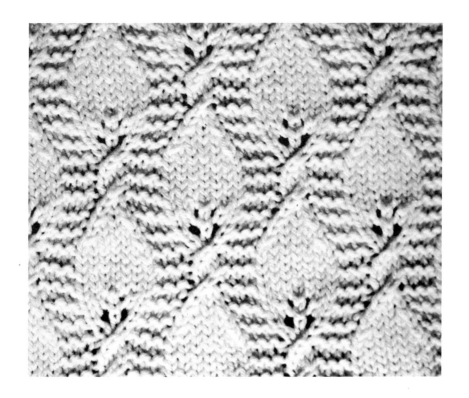

A new variation of the old Victorian leaf. This attractive fabric may be used for almost anything in women's wear and household items.

Suggested uses: Dresses, jackets, pullovers, alternating afghan strips, drapery fabric, winter stoles, mufflers, hats, slipper tops

Cast on a multiple of 16 stitches plus 1.

Row 1: P 2, *k 7, p 3, k 3, p 3*. Repeat between *'s across row → and end last repeat: P 2 (instead of p 3).

Row 2 (and all even-numbered rows): Purl.

Row 3: P 2, *k 7, p 3, twist 3, p 3*. Repeat between *'s across row → and end last repeat: P 2 (instead of p 3).

Row 5: P 2, *sl 1, k 1, psso, k 3, k 2 tog, p 3, k 1, o, k 1, o, k 1, p 3*. Repeat between *'s across row → and end last repeat: P 2 (instead of p 3).

Row 7: P 2, *sl 1, k 1, psso, k 1, k 2 tog, p 3, k 2, o, k 1, o, k 2, p 3*. Repeat between *'s across row → and end last repeat: P 2 (instead of p 3).

Row 9: P 2, *twist 3, p 3, k 7, p 3*. Repeat between *'s and end last repeat: P 2 (instead of p 3).

Row 11: P 2, *k 3, p 3, k 7, p 3*. Repeat between *'s across row and end last repeat: P 2.

Row 13: Same as Row 9.

Row 15: P 2, *k 1, o, k 1, o, k 1, p 3, sl 1, k 1, psso, k 3, k 2 tog, p 3*. Repeat between *'s and end last repeat: P 2.

Row 17: P 2, *k 2, o, k 1, o, k 2, p 3, sl 1, k 1, psso, k 1, k 2 tog, p 3*. Repeat between *'s and end last repeat: P 2.

Row 19: Same as Row 3.

Row 20: Purl.

SHIFT-STROLLER in Cable and Leaf Pattern

Materials required: 7 4-oz skeins 4-ply knitting worsted, 1 ⚹00 crochet hook, 1 pair ⚹7 knitting needles (for ribbed collar and cuffs), and

1 pair ⚹8 knitting needles for size 34–36 or
1 pair ⚹9 knitting needles for size 38–40

Due to the large multiple (16 sts) of Cable and Leaf Pattern, it is not possible to adjust the stitch multiples to be cast on to 1 knitting needle size, inasmuch as a 16-st jump from one size to another would result in the skipping of several sizes. It is necessary, therefore, for large multipled pattern stitches to be adjusted to more than 1 needle size.

Stitch gauge: ⚹8 needles, 9 sts equal 2″.
⚹9 needles, 8½ sts equal 2″.

BACK: Using larger size needles, cast on 81 sts and work in Cable and Leaf Pattern until fabric measures 30″ (or desired length to underarm) from beginning of work.

SHAPE SLEEVES: At beginning of next 4 rows (counting both right and reverse sides as rows) cast on 16 sts. This will total 32 sts on each side for sleeves; 145 sts will now be on needles. Care should be taken to follow pattern stitch after each group of 16 sts have been cast on. Work until fabric measures 38″ from beginning of work (or desired length to underarm, plus 8″). Complete pattern stitch to either Row 10 or Row 20, whichever is reached first, and bind off all sts loosely.

FRONT: Work as for back until fabric measures 35″ from beginning of work (or desired length to underarm plus 5½″). With right side facing, shape neckline as follows: work in pattern across 65 sts. Bind off next 15 sts and work in pattern across remaining sts. Each shoulder and sleeve will now be worked separately. Knit 2 sts tog at neck edge only, every row 8 times, taking care to follow pattern stitch. Work across remaining 57 sts until fabric measures 38" (or desired length to underarm plus 8") from beginning of work, complete pattern to either Row 10 or Row 20 (as for back), and bind off all sts loosely. Attach yarn to neck edge of corresponding side and work the same.

RIBBED COLLAR: Using #7 needles, cast on 160 sts and work in k 1, p 1 ribbing until fabric measures 4½" from beginning. Bind off all sts loosely.

RIBBED CUFF (make 2): Using #7 needles, cast on 60 sts and work in k 1, p 1 ribbing until fabric measures 6½" from beginning. Bind off all sts loosely.

ASSEMBLING AND FINISHING: Sew narrow edges of collar and cuffs tog. Sew shoulder, sleeve, and side seams. Work 1 row of single crochet around neckline and sleeves. Work 2 rows of single crochet around lower edge of shift. Sew collar and cuffs in place, joining the bound-off edges of collar and cuffs to the single crochet edges of neckline and sleeves. Hem to desired length. Block to exact measurements.

CABLE AND DIADEM

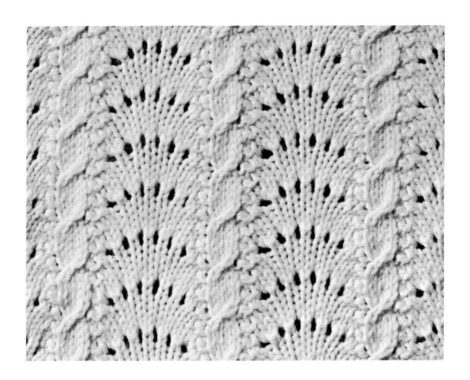

Cast on a multiple of 19 stitches plus 1.

Row 1: *K 6, p 2 tog, k 4, p 2 tog, k 5*. Repeat between *'s across row and end: K 1.
Row 2: Purl.
Row 3: *K 5, p 2 tog, k 4, p 2 tog, k 4*. Repeat between *'s across row, and end: K 1.
Row 4: Purl.
Row 5: K 1, *(o, k 1) 3 times, p 2 tog, twist 4, p 2 tog, k 1, (o, k 1) 3 times*. Repeat between *'s across row.
Row 6: Purl.

ARROW AND CABLE

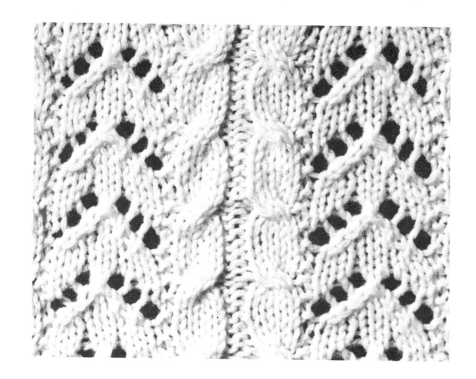

Cast on a multiple of 19 stitches plus 2.

Row 1: *P 2, k 5, o, k 2 tog, k 3, k 2 tog, o, k 5*. Repeat between *'s across row and end: P 2.

Row 2: *K 2, p 4, k 1, p 7, k 1, p 4*. Repeat between *'s across row and end: K 2.

Row 3: *P 2, k 6, o, k 2 tog, k 1, k 2 tog, o, k 6*. Repeat between *'s across row and end: P 2.

Row 4: Same as Row 2.

Row 5: *P 2, cable 4 (2 over 2) right, k 3, o, sl 1, k 2 tog, psso, o, k 3, cable 4 (2 over 2) left*. Repeat between *'s across row and end: P 2.

Row 6: Same as Row 2.

Row 7: *P 2, k 17*. Repeat between *'s across row and end: P 2.

Row 8: Same as Row 2.

BUTTERFLY TWIST

A moderately lacy vertical motif that utilizes the Baby Cable pattern (page 31) in its design.

Suggested uses: Women's wear, afghan strips, stoles, shrugs, place setting mats, drapery and upholstery fabric lined with contrasting color

Cast on a multiple of 19 stitches.

Row 1: *P 1, k 2, p 2, k 2 tog, k 2, o, k 1, o, k 2, sl 1, k 1, psso, p 2, k 2, p 1*. Repeat between *'s across row, taking careful note that each repeat begins and ends with a p 1.

Row 2 (and all even-numbered rows): Purl.

Row 3: *P 1, twist 2, p 2, k 2 tog, k 2, o, k 1, o, k 2, sl 1, k 1, psso, p 2, twist 2, p 1*. Repeat between *'s across row.

Row 5: *P 1, k 2, p 2, k 2 tog, k 1, o, k 3, o, k 1, sl 1, k 1, psso, p 2, k 2, p 1*. Repeat between *'s across row.

Row 7: *P 1, twist 2, p 2, k 2 tog, o, k 5, o, sl 1, k 1, psso, p 2, twist 2, p 1*. Repeat between *'s across row.

Row 8: Purl.

SHELL AND WAVE

A new pattern with a remarkably fragile and delicate appearance, even when knitted with the heavyweight yarns.

Suggested uses: Women's wear, tablecloths, place setting mats, decorative centerpieces, lounge wear, drapery fabric

Cast on a multiple of 12 stitches plus 1.

Row 1: Knit.

Row 2 (right side): Knit a double throw into each st across row.

Row 3: Sl 4 (slip first strand of double throw purlwise onto right needle without working, dropping second strand), slip these 4 sts back onto left needle and knit them all tog as 1 st, *o, (k 1, o) 5 times (knitting first strand and slipping second strand off needle without working), sl 7 purlwise, slip back to left needle and knit them all tog*. Repeat between *'s across row → and end: Sl 4, slip back to left needle, and knit these 4 tog.

Row 4: Knit across row → being careful to knit all overs (o) of previous row as separate sts. → There should be one over (o) BETWEEN each st across row.

Row 5: Knit.

Row 6: Knit.

SPRING AND SUMMER TWOSOME
in Shell and Wave Pattern

Materials required: 7 4-oz skeins 4-ply knitting worsted, 4 pearl buttons ¾" diameter, 1 pair ⚹5 knitting needles (for cuffs and front bands), 1 pair ⚹9 knitting needles for skirt, and an additional pair of knitting needles for the body of the cardigan top, as specified below:

> ⚹6 knitting needles
> for size 36–38
> ⚹7 knitting needles
> for size 40–42

NOTE: It is suggested that materials be purchased at a department store or yarn shop employing a knitting instructor so that assistance can be obtained, if necessary, in making the following article. If a larger or smaller size is needed, or another pattern stitch is desired, assistance and directions for these can also be obtained.

Stitch gauge: ⚹6 needles, 24 sts (2 patterns) equal 4¾".

⚹7 needles, 24 sts (2 patterns) equal 5½".

BACK: Cast on 97 sts and work in Garter Stitch (knit every row) until there are 6 purl ridges on one side of fabric, then work in Shell and Wave Pattern until fabric measures 15" from beginning of work. Work through Row 4 of pattern stitch, and at beginning of Rows 5 and 6 bind off 12 sts (once each side for sleeve insets). Continue working until sleeve insets measure:

> 7½" for size 36–38
> 8" for size 40–42

Complete pattern through Row 5, and on Row 6 bind off all sts loosely.

LEFT FRONT: Cast on 37 sts and work 6 purl ridges (as for back), then work in Shell and Wave Pattern until fabric measures 15" from

144

beginning of work, taking care to count pattern units so that there are the same number on fronts as on back. Complete pattern through Row 5, and at beginning of Row 6, bind off 12 sts. (For RIGHT front, bind off these 12 sts on Row 1.) This is the beginning of sleeve inset. When sleeve inset measures the same as for back, complete pattern through Row 5, and on Row 6 bind off all sts loosely.

Right Front: Make as for left front, except as directed for RIGHT front in parentheses above.

SLEEVE (make 2): Cast on 73 sts and work in Shell and Wave Pattern until fabric measures 12″ from beginning of work. Complete pattern through Row 5 and bind off on Row 6 loosely.

CUFFS: Using ⚞5 needles, and with right side facing, run needle through loops made by cast-on sts at lower edge of sleeve, picking up 73 sts. First row: Knit across, decreasing (k 2 tog) at regular intervals so that the number of sts on needle is reduced to:

46 sts for size 36–38
52 sts for size 40–42

Work in Garter Stitch until there are 7 purl ridges on right side of fabric. Bind off all sts loosely (knitwise) on reverse side of work. Work second sleeve exactly the same.

CENTER FRONT BANDS: Using ⚞5 needles, cast on 15 sts and work in Garter Stitch until there are 21 purl ridges on side facing, counting the "purly" side of cast-on sts as first ridge. **Work buttonhole:** K 7, wind yarn around right needle twice, knit next 2 sts tog, k 6. Next row (reverse side): K 7, knit first strand of yarn, drop second strand from needle, k 7. Continue in Garter Stitch until there are 20 purl ridges above buttonhole, then work the two buttonhole rows once more. Continue in this manner, working a buttonhole between each 20 rows of purl ridges until there are 4 buttonholes in all. Discontinue buttonholes and work in Garter Stitch (only) until band measures:

25″ for size 36–38
25¾″ for size 40–42

from beginning of work. Bind off all sts loosely. This is the right front band. **Left Front Band:** Cast on 15 sts and work in Garter Stitch (only) until band measures the same as right band (each band should contain exactly the same number of purl ridges). Bind off all sts loosely.

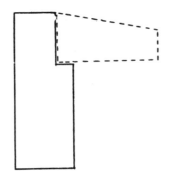

ASSEMBLING AND FINISH-ING: Sew shoulder and side seams. Sew sleeve seams from lower edge to within 2½" from top at underarm. Leave this upper portion of sleeve open. Set sleeve into inset by sewing bind-off edge sts to straight edge across shoulder. Sew the 2½" unsewn seam (at top of sleeve) to underarm bind-off sts of sleeve inset (see drawing).

Sew the 2 center front Garter Stitch bands tog at narrow bind-off edges. Pin this seam at center back of neckline, then pin band down each edge of center front opening, making sure that buttonholes are on right front edge. Sew band to cardigan, beginning at lower edge and up to back of neckline. Sew other side of band in the same manner. Sew buttons on left front to correspond with buttonholes. Block to exact measurements.

SKIRT (make 2; front and back are identical):

Stitch gauge for ⚊9 needles: 8½ sts equal 2".

Using ⚊9 needles cast on
 82 sts for size 36–38 (hip measurement)
 92 sts for size 40–42 (hip measurement)

and work in Stockinette Stitch (knit right side of fabric, purl reverse side), decreasing 1 end st each side every 6" until fabric measures 18" from beginning of work. Continue without decreases until fabric measures 20". Decrease 1 end st each side every inch until fabric measures 28" from beginning. Bind off all sts loosely.

ASSEMBLING AND FINISHING: Sew side seams tog. Sew a ¾" hem at waistline, leaving 1" of this hem unsewn. Cut a piece of ¾"-wide elastic to exact waist measurement PLUS ½". Run this elastic through hem at waistline, overlap ends ½", and sew these ends firmly tog. Sew up the 1" opening left in hem. Turn lower edge of skirt to desired length and hem. Block to exact measurements.

MARINA

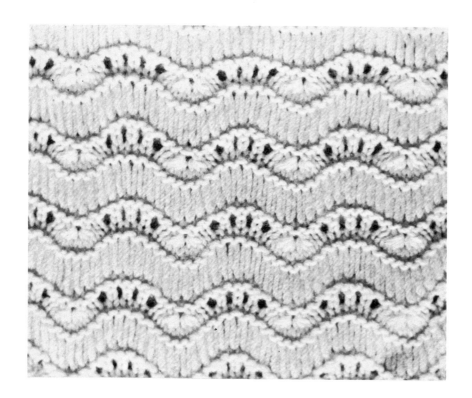

This attractive pattern is a treasure where speed is the prime consideration. This design knits up like lightning and it is possible to make an article of apparel in just a few hours time from start to finish.

Suggested uses: Blouses, stoles, shifts, shrugs, lounge wear, coverlets, bedspreads, draperies, tablecloths, scarves

Cast on a multiple of 11 stitches plus 1.

Row 1: Knit.

Row 2: Purl.

Row 3: K 1, *o, k 1, o, k 1, sl 1, sl 1, k 1, pass these 2 sl sts tog over knit st, k 3 tog, k 1, o, k 1, o, k 1*. Repeat between *'s across row.

Row 4: Knit.

Row 5: Knit a triple throw into each st across row.

Row 6: Knit, knitting first strand of triple throw and dropping second and third.

IV
USEFUL INFORMATION

Creative Form Knitting

A knitter wishing to make a shell or blouse of simple lines, using the pattern stitch or border design of her choice, can do so very easily without a set of specific directions by using the following Creative Form diagrams and their accompanying general directions.

The very simple shapes shown are easily blocked before assembling, and the "straight across" neckline will fall into a slight curve beneath the throat; an example of this is the neckline of Toga Top (see photo) in Section II.

The backs and fronts of these shells and blouses are identical; the knitter makes 2 of each, exactly the same, for the completed garment.

A plain skirt can be made to accompany these tops, in either matching or contrasting yarn, by using the skirt directions portion of Spring and Summer Twosome in Section III.

A charming shift or sheath dress can also be created from the same diagrams by knitting to the desired dress length from lower edge to underarm. Six skeins of yarn will be required for either of these. A 4-strand cord tied at the waist completes the sheath.

Materials required for sleeveless shell, cap-sleeve shell, short-sleeve blouse, and elbow-sleeve blouse: 3 4-oz skeins 4-ply knitting worsted or any yarn of similar weight yielding the required number of stitches per inch, 1 pair of knitting needles ($\#8$, $\#9$, $\#10$) yielding the following stitch gauge: $8\frac{1}{2}$ sts equal 2″. The stitch-gauge swatch should be knitted in the yarn and pattern stitch in which the shell or blouse is to be made.

Size 32	cast	on	72	sts	plus	stitch-multiple	adjustment
″ 34	″	″	76	″	″	″	″	″
″ 36	″	″	81	″	″	″	″	″
″ 38	″	″	85	″	″	″	″	″
″ 40	″	″	90	″	″	″	″	″
″ 42	″	″	95	″	″	″	″	″
″ 44	″	″	99	″	″	″	″	″

For a specific pattern stitch, adjust the above number of sts to the correct multiple by adding or subtracting a few sts to obtain the correct multiple. Only those pattern stitches should be used that require no more than 3 or 4 sts to be added or subtracted. If the knitter wishes to use the exact number of sts given above, with no multiple adjustments involved, she can select a pattern stitch requiring a given number of sts from the pattern substitution chart that immediately follows this chapter.

MAKE 2 (front and back are identical): Work in desired pattern stitch (being sure that the stitch gauge, as specified above, is correct) until fabric measures 14″ (or desired length to underarm) for

sleeveless shell, short-sleeve blouse, elbow-sleeve blouse;

then continue directions as specified under diagrams for each on the following pages. For CAP-SLEEVE shell: Continue in desired pattern stitch until fabric measures 21″ (or desired length from lower edge to shoulder seam) and continue directions under diagram for cap-sleeve shell.

SLEEVELESS SHELL

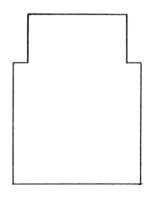

At beginning of next 2 rows, bind off 9 sts (once each side for arm opening), taking care to keep in pattern stitch. (NOTE: 1 or 2 pattern-stitch multiples can be bound off instead of 9 sts, if this number falls within 1 st of 9 either way. For example, if the pattern-stitch multiple is 4, then 8 sts can be bound off; if the pattern-stitch multiple is 10, then 10 sts can be bound off. This will enable the knitter to stay within the exact stitch multiple used.) Continue in pattern until arm openings measure:

7″ for sizes 32, 34, and 36
7½″ for size 38
8″ for all larger sizes

Bind off all sts loosely.

BLOCKING: Before assembling, block each piece to EXACT measurements plus any extra allowance desired.

ASSEMBLING AND FINISHING: Sew shoulder seams, leaving a 10″ opening for neckline. Sew side seams. Two rows of single crochet can be worked around neckline, arm openings, and lower edge if desired. Seams can be lightly pressed on reverse side with steam iron when assembled.

CAP-SLEEVE SHELL

Bind off all sts loosely.

BLOCKING: Before assembling, block each piece to EXACT measurements plus any extra allowance desired.

ASSEMBLING AND FINISHING: Sew shoulder seams, leaving a 10″ opening for neckline. Sew side seams, leaving a

7″ arm opening for sizes 32, 34, and 36
7½″ arm opening for size 38
8″ arm opening for all larger sizes

Two rows of single crochet can be worked around neckline, arm openings, and lower edge if desired. Seams can be lightly pressed on reverse side with steam iron when assembled.

SHORT-SLEEVE BLOUSE

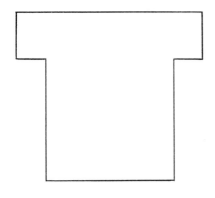

At the beginning of next 2 rows, cast on 9 sts (once each side for sleeves), taking care to keep in pattern stitch. (NOTE: 1 or 2 pattern-stitch multiples can be cast on instead of 9 sts, if this number falls within 1 st of 9 either way. For example: If the pattern-stitch multiple is 5, then 10 sts can be cast on. This will enable the knitter to stay within the exact stitch multiple used.) Continue in pattern until sleeves measure:

7″ for sizes 32, 34, and 36
7½″ for size 38
8″ for all larger sizes

Bind off all sts loosely.

BLOCKING: Before assembling, block each piece to EXACT measurements plus any extra allowance desired.

ASSEMBLING AND FINISHING: Sew shoulder seams, leaving a 10″ opening for neckline. Sew side seams and underarm of sleeves. Two rows of single crochet can be worked around neckline, sleeves, and lower edge if desired. Seams can be lightly pressed on reverse side with steam iron when assembled.

ELBOW-SLEEVE BLOUSE

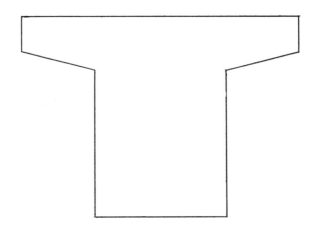

At the beginning of next 8 rows (4 times each side for sleeves) cast on 9 sts, taking care to keep in pattern stitch. (NOTE: 1 or 2 pattern-stitch multiples can be cast on instead of 9 sts, if this number falls within 1 st of 9 either way; or sleeve sts can be cast on at beginning of each row in exact pattern-stitch multiples for desired length of sleeve. This will enable the knitter to stay within the exact stitch multiple used.) When all sleeve sts have been cast on, continue in pattern stitch until sleeve, from underarm to upper edge, measures:

> 7″ for sizes 32, 34, and 36
> 7½″ for size 38
> 8″ for all larger sizes

Bind off all sts loosely.

BLOCKING: Before assembling, block each piece to EXACT measurements plus any extra allowance desired.

ASSEMBLING AND FINISHING: Sew shoulder seams, leaving a 10″ opening for neckline. Sew side seams and underarm of sleeves. Two rows of single crochet can be worked around neckline, sleeves, and lower edge, if desired. Seams can be lightly pressed on reverse side with steam iron when assembled.

Pattern Substitutions

Most of the knitted items pictured can be made in pattern stitches other than the one in which it is shown provided that the knitting needles used are of a PROPER SIZE to yield EXACTLY the SAME STITCH GAUGE that is specified in any given set of directions. This is extremely important. The stitch gauge of any substitute pattern should always be determined BEFORE beginning an article. Pattern stitches may vary tremendously in the number of stitches per inch; for example, slip-cluster patterns such as Treva and Daisy Chain have a tendency to turn out much narrower in width than a solid or lacy knitted fabric; therefore a larger needle is generally needed to obtain a proper stitch count.

In the section entitled "Yarns" a method is given by which a knitter can determine the exact stitch gauge of any given pattern stitch or type of yarn. If a stitch-gauge swatch yields FEWER stitches per inch than are required in a given set of directions, use a SMALLER needle size to obtain the proper number of stitches per inch of fabric. If a stitch-gauge swatch yields MORE stitches than are required, use a LARGER needle size to obtain the proper number of stitches.

The stole (knitted in Signe Pattern) pictured in Section I can be knitted in any of the following substitute patterns, using the same general directions and any needle size yielding the EXACT stitch gauge specified.

Old Shale (cast on 77 stitches)
Dede (cast on 77 stitches)
Double Purl
Jacqueline
Eyelet Band (add 1 extra stitch)
Candlelight (add 1 extra stitch)

Falling Leaf (add 1 extra stitch)
Alpine (add 1 extra stitch)
Diamond Filigree (add 1 extra stitch)
Pyramid (add 1 extra stitch)
Pyramid Lace (add 1 extra stitch)
Marina (cast on 78 stitches)

The girl's cardigan and cap set in Ingrid Pattern pictured in Section I can be knitted in any of the following substitute patterns, using the same general directions and any size needle yielding the EXACT stitch gauge specified.

Isabel
Horizontal Stripe
Madelon
Double Purl

Moss Stitch
Chelsea
Eyelet Band

156

Daisy Chain (take ACCURATE stitch
  gauge)
Frilly Shell (take ACCURATE stitch
  gauge)
Valentine

Pine Tree
Primrose Lace
Shell and Wave
Stockinette

The walking coat for dog or cat in Double Purl Pattern pictured in
Section I can be knitted in the following patterns, following the same
general directions and using any needle size yielding the EXACT stitch
gauge specified.

Horizontal Stripe
Stockinette

Garter Stitch
K 1, P 1 Ribbing

The boat-neck pullover pictured in Section I can be knitted in the
following patterns, using the same general directions and using any size
knitting needle which yields the EXACT stitch gauge specified.

Berry Patch
Horizontal Stripe
Double Moss Stitch

Baby Cable
Cable

The decorator pillow in Frills and Pearls Pattern pictured in Section II
can be knitted in any of the following substitute patterns, using the same
general directions and any needle size which yields the EXACT stitch
gauge specified.

Austrian Puff (add 1 extra stitch)
Horizontal Stripe
Madelon (add 1 extra stitch)
Violet (add 5 extra stitches; pillow
  will be slightly wider than specified
  width)
Daisy (add 5 extra stitches; pillow
  will be slightly wider than specified
  width)

Bridget (add 1 extra stitch)
Lantern (add 1 extra stitch)
Diamond Quilt (add 2 extra stitches)
Doves on the Wing (add 2 extra
  stitches)
Puffin (add 1 extra stitch)

The large needlework bag in Snowdrop Pattern pictured in Section II
can be made in the following patterns, using the same general directions
and any needle size yielding the EXACT stitch gauge specified.

Austrian Puff (add 1 extra stitch)
Madelon (add 1 extra stitch)
Ingrid (add 1 extra stitch)
Cable
Harrison Cable

Bow Knot (add 2 extra stitches)
Frilly Shell (add 1 extra stitch)
Scalloped Shell (add 1 extra stitch)
Embossed Shell (add 1 extra stitch)
Katherine

Tote bags and needlework bags can be made in any desired material
such as "straw"-type yarns, quick-knit crochet cotton, and novelty wool
mixtures provided the specified stitch gauge can be obtained.

The blouse in Candlelight Pattern, with elbow-length sleeves, pictured in Section III, can be made in any of the following patterns, using the same general directions and any needle size yielding the EXACT stitch gauge specified.

Double Purl	Scalloped Shell
Moss Stitch	Embossed Shell
Chelsea	Alpine
Eyelet Band	Diamond Filigree

The luncheon cloth or tablecloth in Rose Leaf Lace Pattern pictured in Section III can be made in any of the following patterns, using the same general directions and any needle size yielding the EXACT stitch gauge specified.

Eyelet Band	Pyramid
Peruvian Lace (add 1 extra stitch)	Pyramid Lace
Falling Leaf	Flower Garden

The place setting mat in Alpine Pattern pictured in Section III can be made in any of the following patterns, using the same general directions and any needle size yielding the EXACT stitch gauge specified.

Baby Diamond (cast on 80 stitches)	Scalloped Shell
Berry Patch (cast on 80 stitches)	Peruvian (cast on 82 stitches)
Basket Weave (cast on 83 stitches)	Candlelight
Chessboard (cast on 83 stitches)	Falling Leaf
Nipper (cast on 82 stitches)	Palm Leaf (cast on 83 stitches)
Donna	Diamond Filigree
Jacqueline (cast on 80 stitches)	Pyramid
Eyelet Band	Pyramid Lace
Bow Knot (cast on 82 stitches)	Flower Garden
Baby Shell (cast on 80 stitches)	Cable and Leaf

This place setting mat can be made in any desired material such as "straw"-type yarns, quick-knit crochet cotton (single strand), and novelty wool mixtures provided the specified stitch gauge can be obtained.

The shift-stroller in Cable and Leaf Pattern pictured in Section III can be made in any of the following patterns, using the same general directions and any needle size yielding the EXACT stitch gauge specified.

Moss Stitch	Falling Leaf
Chelsea	Alpine
Eyelet Band	Diamond Filigree
Tulip Time	Pyramid
Candlelight	Flower Garden

The cardigan top (Spring and Summer Twosome in Shell and Wave Pattern) pictured in Section III can be made in any of the following

158

patterns, using the same general directions and any needle size yielding the EXACT stitch gauge specified.

Isabel

Horizontal Stripe

Madelon

Ingrid

Battersea

Double Purl

Moss Stitch

Chelsea

Eyelet Band

Valentine

Pine Tree

Primrose Lace

Various pattern stitches given in this book can be used with almost any suitable set of directions, depending on the multiple of the desired pattern stitch. The stitch gauge of the chosen pattern stitch should be exactly the same as specified in the directions for the item to be made.

Care should be taken to determine if the set of directions is suitable for pattern-stitch substitution. If directions call for the length of a garment or other item to be measured in inches, other pattern stitches, as a general rule, can be substituted; however, if directions call for the length of an item to be measured by rows or pattern units, pattern-stitch substitutions would not be possible because the number of rows or pattern units to be found in different pattern stitches varies widely.

In any specific set of directions that a knitter may wish to use, if the number of stitches to be cast on is odd (uneven), any of the following pattern stitches can be substituted:

Horizontal Stripe

Double Purl

Moss Stitch

Eyelet Band

Stockinette

Garter Stitch

Chelsea

If the number of stitches to be cast on is even (divisible by 2), the following pattern stitches can be substituted:

Horizontal Stripe

Double Purl

Stockinette

Garter Stitch

K1, P1 Ribbing

A knitter can determine which pattern stitch can be substituted in any suitable set of directions by using the following chart. First, find the name of the pattern stitch to be substituted in the list at the left. If the correct number of stitches to be cast on (in the set of directions to be used) appears in the group of numbers opposite this pattern stitch, then it can be used to knit the desired item. If the correct number of stitches does not appear at the right of the chosen pattern stitch, then it should not be used, and the knitter should select another appropriate pattern stitch in another group.

For example: If a specific set of directions calls for 88 stitches to be cast on and the knitter wishes to use Old Shale (instead of the pattern specified in the directions) she first finds Old Shale in the list of pattern names. If the number of stitches to be cast on (88) can be found at the right of the group in which Old Shale appears, then this pattern can be used. The number 88 may also appear in several other groups of pattern stitches, so that one set of directions can be used to make several items of the same design but of different pattern stitches.

Berry Patch Double Moss Stitch Baby Cable	4, 8, 12, 16, 20, 24, 28, 32, 36, 40, 44, 48, 52, 56, 60, 64, 68, 72, 76, 80, 84, 88, 92, 96, 100, 104, 108, 112, 116, 120, 124, 128, 132, 136, 140, 144, 148, 152
Battersea	5, 9, 13, 17, 21, 25, 29, 33, 37, 41, 45, 49, 53, 57, 61, 65, 69, 73, 77, 81, 85, 89, 93, 97, 101, 105, 109, 113, 117, 121, 125, 129, 133, 137, 141, 145, 149, 153
Nipper Peruvian Peruvian Lace	6, 10, 14, 18, 22, 26, 30, 34, 38, 42, 46, 50, 54, 58, 62, 66, 70, 74, 78, 82, 86, 90, 94, 98, 102, 106, 110, 114, 118, 122, 126, 130, 134, 138, 142, 146, 150, 154
Madelon Lantern Lacy Daisy Painted Daisy Daisy Chain Treva Frilly Shell	7, 13, 19, 25, 31, 37, 43, 49, 55, 61, 67, 73, 79, 85, 91, 97, 103, 109, 115, 121, 127, 133, 139, 145, 151
Baby Diamond Vertical Stripe Baby Shell Lacy Shell Diamond Quilt Doves on the Wing	8, 14, 20, 26, 32, 38, 44, 50, 56, 62, 68, 74, 80, 86, 92, 98, 104, 110, 116, 122, 128, 134, 140, 146, 152
Lattice Checker	9, 15, 21, 27, 33, 39, 45, 51, 57, 63, 69, 75, 81, 87, 93, 99, 105, 111, 117, 123, 129, 135, 141, 147, 153
Lilith Lacy Cable	7, 14, 21, 28, 35, 42, 49, 56, 63, 70, 77, 84, 91, 98, 105, 112, 119, 126, 133, 140, 147, 154
Signe Diagonal Jacqueline	8, 16, 24, 32, 40, 48, 56, 64, 72, 80, 88, 96, 104, 112, 120, 128, 136, 144, 152

Tulip Time Falling Leaf Pyramid Pyramid Lace	9, 17, 25, 33, 41, 49, 57, 65, 73, 81, 89, 97, 105, 113, 121, 129, 137, 145, 153
Donna	9, 18, 27, 36, 45, 54, 63, 72, 81, 90, 99, 108, 117, 126, 135, 144, 153
Bows in Rows Violet Daisy Dragonfly Border Spring Posy Border Scalloped Shell Embossed Shell Candlelight Alpine Diamond Filigree	11, 21, 31, 41, 51, 61, 71, 81, 91, 101, 111, 121, 131, 141, 151, 161, 171
Andrea Bow Knot	12, 22, 32, 42, 52, 62, 72, 82, 92, 102, 112, 122, 132, 142, 152, 162
Basket Weave	13, 23, 33, 43, 53, 63, 73, 83, 93, 103, 113, 123, 133, 143, 153, 163
Old Shale Dede Frills and Pearls	11, 22, 33, 44, 55, 66, 77, 88, 99, 110, 121, 132, 143, 154, 165
Austrian Puff Eyelet Chevron Monique Marina	12, 23, 34, 45, 56, 67, 78, 89, 100, 111, 122, 133, 144, 155, 166
Katherine	12, 24, 36, 48, 60, 72, 84, 96, 108, 120, 132, 144, 156, 168
Isabel Ingrid Valentine Pine Tree Primrose Lace Shell and Wave	13, 25, 37, 49, 61, 73, 85, 97, 109, 121, 133, 145, 157, 169

Pattern Stitch Knitting for Beginners

The most painless way to learn intricate lace pattern-stitch knitting is to sneak up on it, one stitch at a time, beginning with the over (o) and the simplest of all decreases (k 2 tog). Below are 5 simple exercises by which a beginning knitter can learn to do the basic and most often employed stitches in lacy or openwork knitting.

[1] Using medium- or heavyweight yarn and large needles, cast on 12 sts and purl across 1 row, then repeat the 2 following rows, counting the sts on needle after each purl row:

Row 1: *K 1, o, k 2 tog*. Repeat between *'s across row.
Row 2: Purl across reverse side, purling each over (o) as a separate st.

With very few exceptions, most lacy patterns maintain the same number of sts in each row. You will soon see a very simple eyelet-ladder pattern beginning to take shape, providing the 12 sts are maintained across each row. Continue with this knitting exercise until you have knitted 2 or 3" of fabric without errors and without further reference to the printed directions.

[2] Cast on 16 sts and purl across the first row.

Row 1: *K 1, o, k 1, sl 1, k 1, psso*. Repeat between *'s across row, referring to General Instructions if necessary, for specific directions for working a sl 1 and a psso (pass slip stitch over knit stitch).
Row 2: Purl across row, purling each over (o) as a separate st.

Repeat these 2 rows until you have knitted 2 or 3" of fabric without errors and without further reference to the printed directions.

[3] Cast on 14 sts and purl across the first row.
Repeat Rows 1 and 2 of Baby Diamond Pattern (Section I) and proceed until these 2 rows can be knitted without further reference to printed directions.

[4] Cast on 20 sts and work all 4 rows of Baby Diamond Pattern, repeating until no further reference to printed directions is necessary.

[5] Cast on 23 sts and work in Eyelet Chevron Pattern (Section I) and work until no further reference to printed directions is necessary.

When you have completed these 5 simple patterns without errors and from memory after the first few rows, you should have the "feel" of lacy pattern-stitch knitting. Before beginning an item in a very intricate lacy stitch, make a simple article in a simple pattern, such as a scarf in Lilith Pattern (Section I), as follows:

Materials required: 3 1-oz balls 2-ply Mohair Blend or any yarn yielding the stitch gauge below, and 1 pair ⚹8 knitting needles.

Stitch gauge: 14 sts equal 3".

Cast on 49 sts and knit across 6 rows, then work in Lilith Pattern until scarf measures approximately 45" from beginning, and end on Row 4 of pattern. Knit across 5 rows, then bind off all sts (knitwise) on reverse side loosely. Steam press lightly on reverse side.

Yarns

Most of the knitted items in this book have been made of 4-ply knitting worsted for two reasons. One is that this yarn is an ideal weight for a knitter to work with; it is not too heavy to make a delicate-looking fabric for a blouse, nor is it too fine to make a good, substantial cardigan for warmth. It can be controlled, by the pattern stitch and the size of the needles used, to the extent that almost anything can be knitted of it. The second and more important reason is that 4-ply knitting worsted is almost universally uniform and available to the knitter wherever she may be.

This is not to imply that other yarns are not desirable as knitting material; however, these may vary from place to place or from yarn company to yarn company. Fingering yarn, for example, may be 2-ply and very fine under one label, and 3-ply (hence thicker) under another. Sports yarn, so called, may be as fine as baby wool in one place and as thick as knitting worsted somewhere else. Sock and sweater yarn (?) is a nebulous term for several kinds of yarn that may vary considerably, depending upon where one resides or what label it is sold under.

The yarn known as Germantown varies much less than most other types; as a general rule, it can be used in place of knitting worsted provided it is of the same thickness, and 4-ply, when used as a substitute, and not of the "featherweight" variety.

Then there are the novelty yarns of which, in a great many instances, the less said the better. Many of these are very attractive, but when they contain less than 50 per cent wool are extremely unpredictable. Many are made totally of synthetic fibers, each one of which reacts in a different way when dry-cleaned or laundered. Where wool remains much the same size when dry-cleaned or carefully washed, one is never quite sure how any of the synthetic fibers will react. A knitted fabric of one of these may yield a stitch gauge of 5 stitches to the inch while still on a pair of knitting needles, and when cleaned or laundered may stretch to 3 or 4 stitches to an inch of fabric, making a garment that was meant to be a size 34 suddenly become a size 38 or 40. Pure mohair yarn is also inclined to react in this way.

This can be overcome by blocking an article before it is assembled. Then, if a suspicion arises that it will turn out larger than planned, the seams can be sewn with the right sides of the fabric together, using a running stitch, in the same manner as one would sew together a garment of woven material. The seams can be sewn together as wide as desired, in order to take up the extra width. Sometimes there is extra length as well; this can be taken up by hemming the garment to the desired length, again in the same manner as one would turn a hem of woven material.

A good rule to follow when using yarns of mohair or synthetic fibers is to consult one's local knitting instructor. She is usually well versed in the use and reactions of these yarns and will oversee the knitting project to its completion.

Silk, linen, and cotton knitting yarns are heavier than wools or synthetics, and a finished article made of these materials almost always has a tendency to be longer and narrower than anticipated, when an unblocked stitch gauge is taken. A vigorously laundered swatch of these materials, however, will usually reveal the true stitch gauge.

When a garment is to be made of any washable material, knit a swatch that will measure at least 5 inches across the needles, using the same size needles as the planned item will be made from, and knitting enough of the desired pattern stitch so that it will be at least 5 or 6″ long. Bind off all stitches loosely and wash this swatch in lukewarm suds, letting it soak a few minutes so that any sizing or other temporary finish intended to create bulk will be washed away. Rinse twice in warm water and allow to dry on a hard, flat surface. When thoroughly dry, press lightly on reverse side with a steam iron or under a damp cloth, then again allow it to dry thoroughly while lying flat. This laundered and pressed swatch will reveal the true stitch gauge, which may be considerably different from what it was on the needles.

When measuring a stitch gauge from a generous swatch of knitted fabric, it is advisable to measure across a 2 or 3″ area so that the gauge will be an average one.

For ultimate beauty in intricate pattern-stitch knitting, it is well for the. knitter to avoid the use of "busy" yarns; that is, those yarns that contain knots, bumps, chunks, loops, repeat formulae, or more than one color. These include yarns known as bouclé, nubby, tweed, and a myriad of others having no common name but many trade names, distinctive products of many yarn companies, all colorfully christened with catchword names sounding like: Tweedee Twirl, Knotty Knymph, Bubble Fuzz, Knubbee Knittee, Blurbalon, British Bumpkin, etc., etc. This, of course, is a fanciful list, but knitters will recognize the real ones from it, and they are endless.

These nubs, chunks, knots, tweeds, and bumps invariably detract from an embossed or lacy pattern stitch, and often seem to be "fighting" with the fabric design. When a knitted garment has too many things going for it, it is just too "busy"-looking. When a knitter takes the trouble to create a beautiful lacy or embossed fabric design, let this stand alone;

166

color, yarn texture, and even styling should be only background effect that will enhance the knitted design. Even bright, primitive colors will obscure the pattern stitch. The most desirable colors for dramatic fabric designs or delicate lacy patterns are white, beige, black, pastels, and muted medium tones. Brilliant scarlets, wild greens, dyspeptic yellows, and blatant blues are attractive and interesting in a native rug purchased on the road to Xochimilco, but horrendous when used in intricate hand-knit fabric designs. Avoid these, and all other things that will detract in any way from your creative handwork.

Knitting Aids and Implements

Probably the most inexpensive commodities on the market today are the tools of the knitter. For as little as a few cents each, one can purchase all sorts of aids to make knitting faster and easier and no knitter should be without these basics. There are also, of course, a lot of interesting gadgets that the knitter may use only occasionally or not at all. The basics, however, such as a good range of knitting-needle sizes, yarn needles, etc., should be considered necessary and kept near at hand for more enjoyable knitting.

Following is a list of knitting aids and implements that every knitter, including the beginner, should acquire. Most knitters will have at least some of the items listed. It is suggested that items listed below that the knitter does not already have should be added to the work basket as soon as possible.

Knitting needles, straight plastic, one pair each of the following sizes: 5, 6, 7, 8, 9, 10, and 10½.

Plastic or metal knitting ruler with stitch-gauge window.

Plastic and metal yarn needles of several sizes.

Cable needle (cable-stitch holder).

Crochet hooks, one each of the following sizes: 1, 0, 00, F, and G.

Stitch holders in at least 2 sizes.

Two pairs of scissors: 1 pair large cutting size and 1 pair small embroidery size.

Small pincushion

Blocking board

Rustproof pins (for use in blocking).

Metal tape measure

General Instructions
with Abbreviation Guide

(Abbreviations and symbols, as used throughout, are noted in parentheses.)

ARROW (→)

This arrow indicates that an unusual procedure, an innovation or a deviation from the usual is to follow. Note carefully all directions and instructions following this arrow before proceeding.

ASTERISK (*)

A symbol used before and after a set of directions that is to be repeated across a row of knitting or crochet. For example: "*K 1, p 2*. Repeat between *'s across row" would be an instruction to knit 1, purl 2 across an entire row. Wording following this symbol is often varied, such as "Repeat from * to *." This instruction would be carried out exactly the same.

BIND OFF

Knit 2 stitches as usual, then with the point of left needle lift first stitch knitted over second stitch, and off the point of right needle; knit another stitch and lift the previously knitted stitch over this one. Repeat this procedure until as many stitches are bound off as are specified in directions.

BLOCKING

Wearing Apparel: Blocking assembled apparel of complicated styling at home is, at best, a hazardous and highly involved operation, and a full and comprehensive text on this procedure is to be found in many good books written expressly to acquaint the knitter with fundamentals, technical aspects, and other nonartistic phases of knitting. Space prevents minute and exhaustive details of this nature in a book dealing mainly with the art of pattern-stitch knitting, and without these details the rudiments would only serve to confuse. It is suggested, therefore, that the knitter either study one of the technical books or have her knitted apparel blocked by a reputable dry-cleaning establishment that specializes in hand-knit blocking.

Simple Shapes: Blocking simple shapes, such as pillows, place setting mats, or unassembled pieces of apparel of simple design, is an entirely different matter from the blocking of assembled wearing apparel—and

169

much simpler. Any item of simple and uncomplicated design can be blocked in the following manner: Before blocking, item should be either steamed or (if washable) wet thoroughly in lukewarm water. To steam, hold steam iron about ½″ from fabric and slowly move iron over entire surface until item is dampened and pliable. If item is immersed in water, lift out of water using both hands (never pick up wet knitted fabric by an edge or corner) and gently squeeze excess moisture out without wringing or twisting. Roll in a terry-cloth towel and leave for a few minutes, so that the absorbent toweling can take up additional moisture. Unroll and remove from towel, again using both hands to lift the wet item. Place the steamed or wet item on a blocking board. A blocking board can be a kitchen cutting board, an old card table into which pins can be pushed, a large piece of fiberboard, etc., that has been spread with terry-cloth toweling. Using a tape measure, gently smooth out the wet or steamed item to the exact desired measurements and pin firmly to the blocking board, using only rustproof pins. Allow item to dry thoroughly, 24 to 36 hours, before removing. If directions call for pieces of an item to be blocked before completion, remove from the blocking board and complete as directed.

CABLE STITCH

This is done with the aid of a cable needle or crochet hook. When directions read "Cable next 4 sts (2 over 2)" proceed as follows: Slip first 2 stitches off left needle onto cable needle or crochet hook, hold to back of work, knit next 2 stitches, pick up cable needle and knit these 2 stitches onto right knitting needle. This completes a right-cross cable stitch. When a left-cross cable stitch is desired, hold the 2 stitches on cable needle to front of work and complete as above. If directions call for next 6 stitches to be cabled (3 over 3), slip 3 stitches off left needle onto cable needle, knit next 3 stitches, then knit the 3 stitches off cable needle onto right knitting needle, holding cable needle to front or back, according to whether a right or left cross is desired.

CAST ON

When casting on stitches to begin an article, it is suggested that the following method be used: Pull out approximately 12″ of yarn for every 10 stitches to be cast on, and place this free end to your left and the skein of yarn to your right. Make a slip loop at this point and place it on knitting needle. Holding needle in right hand and using free end of yarn, loop yarn around thumb or forefinger of left hand, insert needle into this loop, bring skein end of yarn under and over needle, and draw this yarn through loop on left hand. Pull free end of yarn to the left to tighten loop on needle. Repeat this procedure until desired number of loops (including slip loop) have been cast on.

To cast on stitches at the beginning of a row (as for knitted-in sleeves, etc.) on an article already in the process of being knitted, proceed as follows: Insert right needle into first stitch on left needle, as if to knit; yarn over and draw loop through (as in a usual knit stitch) but do not slip this stitch off left needle; instead, slip the loop just knitted from right needle onto left needle, then repeat, inserting right needle into stitch just made, until desired number of stitches have been added. Casting onto needles to begin an article can be done in this same way, making a slip loop over left needle as first stitch.

CORD, twisted 4-strand

For every 7½" of cord needed, measure 1 yd of yarn; for example, if a 30" cord is needed, use a 4-yd strand of yarn. Fold in half and place the 2 cut ends together. Place this folded end over doorknob or have someone hold it firmly. Twist these 2 cut ends to the right (clockwise) until the strands are tightly twisted and appear to be a single strand. Holding the cut ends firmly together, grasp cord in the middle and again fold in half, holding the 2 free ends and again placing the folded end over doorknob, etc. Now twist the 2 free ends to the left (counterclockwise) until cord is tightly twisted. Tie a firm single knot in free end, remove other end from holder, and tie a firm single knot in folded end. Trim ends to ½" from knots.

CORD, twisted 8-strand

For a larger cord, approximately twice the diameter of a 4-strand cord, cut 2 strands of yarn of desired length (instead of one, as in 4-strand cord) and proceed exactly as for the 4-strand twisted cord, using these 2 strands together as one.

CROCHET (cr)

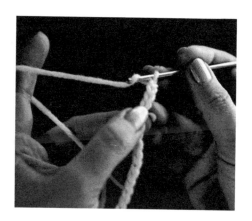

Chain (ch): Place skein or ball of working yarn to your left and make a slip loop about 1½" from end of yarn. With left palm up, place yarn (about 4" below slip loop) down through space between little finger and ring finger, around little finger, then down through space between middle finger and forefinger. Now bring yarn up around forefinger and grasp slip loop between thumb and middle finger.

Insert crochet hook through loop, catch working yarn with hook, and draw through. Again catch working yarn and draw through loop (2 chains made). Continue in this manner, drawing working yarn through each loop formed until desired number of chains have been made, or until

171

chain is of the desired length. Allow working yarn to slide freely through fingers.

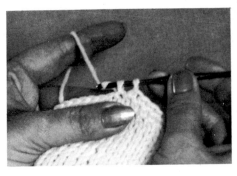

Single Crochet (sgl cr) on knitted edge: With right side of knitted fabric facing, draw working yarn through 2 edge strands of knitted fabric at starting point and tie firmly. With yarn threaded through fingers of left hand (as described in directions for making a chain) insert hook through these same 2 edge strands and draw working yarn through (1 loop on hook), grasp yarn with hook, and draw through loop, *Insert hook through next 2 edge strands of knitted fabric (directly to the left) and draw working yarn through. There will now be 2 loops on hook. Grasp working yarn with hook and draw through both of these loops, leaving 1 loop on hook*. Repeat between *'s for each single crochet, continuing this procedure for desired length of knitted-fabric edge. If crocheted edge ends at a corner or angle of knitted fabric, break yarn 2″ from last single crochet made and draw this end through loop and pull to tighten. If crocheted edge ends at the starting point (first single crochet made), then join these 2 single crochets (first and last made) with a slip stitch (sl st) as follows: Insert hook in top of first single crochet made, grasp working yarn with hook, and draw through both strands of single crochet and loop on hook. Break yarn and pull through loop, if only 1 row of single crochet is called for in specific directions. If more than 1 row is required, do not break yarn after joining with slip stitch, but continue working single crochet stitches in top of each single crochet made on previous row. NOTE: If crocheted edge does not lie flat but ruffles along the knitted fabric edge, a smaller crochet hook should be used. If crocheted edge is too tight and causes the knitting to ruffle, a larger crochet hook should be used.

Crocheted Buttonholes, on knitted edge: Work as many rows of single crochet along knitted edge as are called for in specific directions. On buttonhole row, work as follows: Measure buttons to be used to determine their diameter in inches or fractions thereof; determine how many buttons are to be used and where they will be placed; then on opposite edge (buttonholes are worked on the right front edge of women's wear and on the left front edge of men's wear) mark place where each buttonhole is to be worked by placing 2 straight pins at these points, leaving a space be-

172

tween each pair of pins that is the exact diameter of buttons to be used. Work a single crochet in the top of each single crochet (made on previous

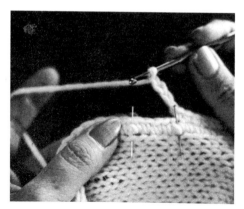 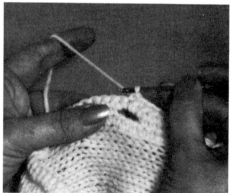

row) until a pair of pins is reached; then make a crochet chain the exact length of the space between pins, single crochet in next stitch directly to the left of second pin and in each stitch thereafter until the next pair of pins is reached. Pins can be removed after each buttonhole chain is worked. Continue this procedure until all buttonholes have been made and end of row has been reached. On next row, work a single crochet in the top of each single crochet (made on previous row) until a buttonhole is reached.

Work as many single crochets in this chain as were skipped on previous row. For example, if button width (between pins) spanned 3 single crochets, then work 3 single crochets through buttonhole chain. Continue in this manner until row has been completed, continuing as directed for specific item.

DECREASE

The most common decrease is made by knitting or purling 2 stitches together. This is a single decrease. Specific directions for working other single, double, and multiple decreases will be found in each specific set of directions.

DIRECTIONS IN PARENTHESES, such as "(k 1, o) 3 times"

Work directions that appear in parentheses as many times as called for immediately following the parenthesized directions. This is not a repeat direction; it is to be worked the exact number of times stated.

GARTER STITCH

Knit each stitch across every row. This creates a reversible fabric consisting of horizontal purl ridges.

INCREASE

Closed Increase: Insert right needle into the stitch directly below next stitch on left needle and knit it, then knit the stitch on left needle (from which the increase was made) as usual.

Cast-On Increase: Cast on 1 stitch at beginning of row and knit the row as usual.

Double Closed Increase: Increase 1 stitch to the right of next stitch (a closed increase; see **Closed Increase),** k 1 (this is the stitch from which the closed increase has just been made), then increase 1 stitch to the left of this stitch, as follows: Insert left needle behind stitch just knitted, and into the same lower stitch as for first increase, lift up, and knit another stitch into it. Three stitches are now on right needle (instead of only 1) as a result of this action.

Lift-Increase: Insert left needle (from front to back) into the yarn running between stitches, then knit or purl this extra stitch according to specific directions.

Open Increase: See **Over (o)**

KNIT (k)

Insert right needle into stitch (loop) nearest the point of left needle, from front to back (keeping working yarn to the back of work); wind working yarn around point of right needle,

then draw yarn (with point of right needle) through loop on left needle and at the same time, slip left loop (just worked) off left needle. Slip the stitch (loop) just made well back (off the point) and onto the body of the right needle.

KNITTING NEEDLES, comparative sizes

AMERICAN	# 0	1	2	3	4	5	6	7	8	9	10	10½	11	13	15
ENGLISH	#13	12	11	10	9	8	7	6	5	4	3		2		

MONTAGE knitting

This group of pattern stitches was designed by the author especially for this book and includes the fabric designs called Bows in Rows, Daisy, Violet, Frills and Pearls, Spring Posy, and Dragonfly. The background is the Garter Stitch, in which every row is knitted, and the Montage is worked into the fabric at designated intervals, with the aid of a single knot, a square knot, and the simple actions of the yarn known as 3-throw, 4-throw, and 5-throw.

OVER (o)

Knitted openwork patterns are based on the over (or yarn over, as it is sometimes called) and the decrease, distributed throughout a knitted fabric in such a manner as to create a lacy filet or filigree design. This action creates an extra stitch in the next row, with a small round hole or eyelet directly beneath it. These eyelets, spaced in various positions, form the basis of the lacy knitted pattern stitch. These added eyelet stitches are always counterbalanced by decreases in direct proportion to the number of overs one creates in a given pattern. This is necessary so that the number of stitches originally cast on will remain the same.

Work an over before a knit stitch as follows: Bring yarn forward between the points of the 2 needles (in the same manner as the yarn is brought forward before working a purl stitch) and place it over the right needle at the back of work. From this (rather peculiar) position, knit the next stitch or stitches according to directions.

Work an over before a purl stitch as follows: With yarn in purl position, wrap it once around the right needle and bring between points of needles, back again to purl position. Purl next stitch or stitches according to directions.

PASS SLIP STITCH OVER KNIT STITCH (psso)

With point of left needle, lift slipped stitch over knitted stitch and off the point of right needle.

PELLON, Iron-On type

This product enables the knitter to put a firm yet pliable backing on knitted fabrics when such a backing is needed. It can be purchased in most yardage shops and department stores. To bond Iron-On Pellon to the back of a knitted fabric, set dry iron to wool temperature. Pin Pellon to reverse side of knitted fabric, using as few pins as possible to hold Pellon in place and making sure that the bonded side (shiny) is against the knitted fabric and the dull or right side is up. Place item on ironing board, Pellon side up; iron the Pellon very slowly, beginning at one side and continuing in a steady movement across fabric, using only slight pressure and avoiding ironing over the pins. Let Pellon cool for a few seconds, then remove pins and repeat this procedure, paying particular attention to edges and corners. Allow bonded fabric to lie flat for several minutes to cool and set. Bonded Pellon is hand launderable when fabric to which it is bonded is also launderable. It is suggested that a small piece of Iron-On Pellon and a small swatch of knitted material be done as practice.

PURL (p)

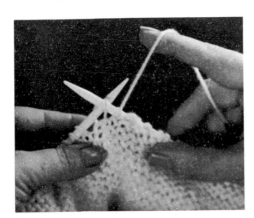

With working yarn at front of work, insert right needle into stitch (loop) nearest the point of left needle (from back to front) and wind working yarn around point of right needle (from right to left),

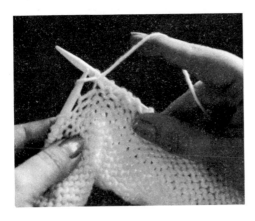

then draw yarn (with point of right needle) through loop on left needle, and at the same time, slip left loop (just worked) off left needle, and slip loop just made well back (off the point) and onto body of right needle. Continue in this manner, keeping working yarn to front of work, if all stitches across this row are to be purled. If a purl stitch is to be made between two knit stitches, the working yarn is brought forward for the purled stitch (between the points of the needles) and then returned to the back of the work for the next knit stitches.

SINGLE KNOT

Bring end of right loop over and under left loop, then pull loops firmly in opposite directions.

176

SLIP (sl)

The action of slipping a stitch (loop) from left needle to right needle without working. This is done knitwise throughout the directions in this book unless purlwise is specifically stated. Generally speaking, a stitch is slipped knitwise when it is to be passed over the next knit stitch, and slipped purlwise when it is to remain in sequence between other stitches across a row. Insert right needle into stitch to be slipped, but instead of knitting or purling this stitch, slide it onto right needle without further action, and continue across row according to specific directions. If more than one stitch is slipped, these should be done separately, as above, unless otherwise specified. The position of the working yarn is not changed when slipping a stitch purlwise unless specifically stated in directions.

SLIP-CLUSTER

This easy and fascinating stitch is the basis of the new fabric designs called Lacy Daisy, Painted Daisy, Andrea, Daisy Chain, and Treva. A slip-cluster is made from a specified number of long stitches made on the previous row by working triple throws, with 1 or more regular knit stitches between as "anchors." To work a slip-cluster, *yarn forward between points of needles, insert right needle purlwise into the first strand (of triple throw) WITHOUT working, and slip from left needle onto right needle (creating a long stitch that has been SLIPPED). Repeat this until specified number of slipped long stitches are on right needle, then take yarn (between points of needles) to back of work, slip all the long stitches back onto left needle, yarn forward (between points of needles) slip long stitches onto right needle, yarn to back (between points of needles), slip long stitches to left needle, yarn forward (between points of needles) slip long stitches to right needle, yarn to back of work* and a slip-cluster has been made. Repeat between *'s for each slip-cluster called for in specific directions (such as: "Slip-cluster next 5 sts").

SLIP LOOP

A loop used for beginning crochet, cast-on stitches, etc. Draw about 6″ of yarn from skein and fold in half. Twist folded end once to the right, then draw skein end of the yarn through this loop (made by right twist). Pull free end of yarn downward to tighten and reduce slip loop to desired size.

SQUARE KNOT

A square knot consists of 2 single knots (see **Single Knot),** the second of which is simply tied in the opposite direction from the first. Bring end of right loop over and under left loop, pulling ends firmly in opposite directions, then bring end of left loop over and under right loop, pulling the ends of these loops firmly in opposite directions until a snug knot is formed between loops.

STITCH(ES) (st, sts)

A pattern stitch, fabric design, or any separate action of a knitting needle called for in the execution of a knitted fabric. Also, loops made by casting onto a knitting needle, an action executed with a crochet hook, an action executed with an embroidery needle, etc.

STOCKINETTE STITCH

Also called stocking stitch, smooth knitting, plain knitting, tricot, Rechts-muster, etc. Knit each stitch across each row on front of fabric, and purl each stitch across each row on reverse side of fabric.

THROW

A throw is used in working various knitted fabric designs and is done by "throwing" or wrapping the yarn around the right needle, according to specific directions.

Double Throw, knitted: Insert needle into stitch as if to knit, wrap yarn around needle 2 times and complete as for a knit stitch.

Double Throw, purled: Insert needle into stitch as if to purl, wrap yarn around needle 2 times and complete as for a purl stitch.

 Triple Throw, knitted or purled: Work as for double throw, wrapping yarn around needle 3 times.

NOTE: A double throw or a triple throw is ALWAYS knitted or purled INTO a stitch, differing from a 3-throw, 4-throw, or 5-throw (see below) which is worked BETWEEN stitches.

3-Throw: Bring working yarn between points of needles from knit position at back, around right needle and again to the back, 3 times. Each time yarn passes between points of needles is counted as one throw. A 3-throw is ALWAYS done BETWEEN stitches.

4-Throw: Bring working yarn through points of needles 4 times, in exactly the same manner as for a 3-throw, above. A 4-throw is ALWAYS done BETWEEN stitches.

5-Throw: Bring working yarn through points of needles 5 times, in exactly the same manner as for a 3-throw or 4-throw, above. A 5-throw is ALWAYS done BETWEEN stitches.

Dropping a 3-throw, 4-throw, or 5-throw on next row: Slide these strands, which were wound around needle on previous row, from left needle and to front of work; these form loops on front of knitted fabric which will be tied when row has been completed. (See **Montage knitting.**)

TOGETHER (tog)

A term used in specific types of decreases.

TWIST 2

Knit into 2 stitches as if knitting the 2 together, draw yarn through, but before slipping from left needle, again knit the stitch nearest to the point of needle, then slip both these stitches off left needle; 2 stitches have now been knitted onto the right needle as a result of this action. This stitch is actually a miniature cable, the uppermost stitch slanting to the right. Where directions do not specify whether the top stitch of the twist should be slanted to the left or to the right, it is this action that is usually called for; it is also exactly the same action when directions specify: "Twist 2 right."

TWIST 2 RIGHT

See **Twist 2,** above.

TWIST 2 LEFT

Knit into back of second stitch from point of left needle, draw yarn through, and knit into first stitch. Slip both these stitches together from left needle; 2 stitches have now been knitted onto the right needle as a result of this action. The uppermost stitch of these 2 slants to the left in a miniature cable.

TWIST 3

Knit into 3 stitches as if knitting them together, draw yarn through, but before slipping from left needle, knit the stitch nearest the point of left needle and slip off needle; then again knit the stitch nearest the point of the left needle and slip off needle. Now slip the last stitch of these 3 off left needle, without knitting it. There will now be 3 stitches on right needle as a result of this action. The uppermost stitch of these 3 will slant to the right in a cable motif.

TWIST 4

Insert right needle into 4 stitches, as if to knit them together, draw yarn through but do not slip from left needle; then knit first 3 stitches on left needle (one at a time) beginning with the stitch nearest the point of needle, slipping each stitch off left needle as it is knitted. Slip the fourth stitch off left needle without working. There will now be 4 stitches on right needle as a result of this action. The uppermost stitch of these 4 will slant to the right in a cable motif.